THE SMALL PUBLIC LIBRARY SURVIVAL GUIDE

Thriving on Less

Herbert B. Landau

AMERICAN LIBRARY ASSOCIATION

Chicago   2008

Herbert B. Landau is director of the Milanof-Schock Library in Mount Joy, Pennsylvania. He has over thirty years of experience in libraries and in the management, publishing, and marketing of scholarly and professional information in both electronic and conventional formats. In 2005 and 2006 the Milanof-Schock Library received the AARP's Award of Excellence for Library Services for Older Adults, and in 2006 the library was named the Best Small Library in America by *Library Journal* and the Bill and Melinda Gates Foundation. Landau has published more than a hundred papers in the library and scholarly press, and he writes a regular news and commentary column for the *Donegal Ledger* newspaper. He holds a B.A. in chemistry from Hunter College and an M.S. from the Columbia University School of Library Service.

While extensive effort has gone into ensuring the reliability of information appearing in this book, the publisher makes no warranty, express or implied, on the accuracy or reliability of the information, and does not assume and hereby disclaims any liability to any person for any loss or damage caused by errors or omissions in this publication.

The paper used in this publication meets the minimum requirements of American National Standard for Information Sciences—Permanence of Paper for Printed Library Materials, ANSI Z39.48-1992. ∞

Library of Congress Cataloging-in-Publication Data
Landau, Herbert B.
   The small public library survival guide : thriving on less / Herbert B. Landau.
      p. cm.
   Includes bibliographical references and index.
   ISBN 978-0-8389-3575-0 (alk. paper)
   1. Public libraries—United States—Administration. 2. Small libraries—United States—Administration. 3. Libraries and community—United States. 4. Library finance—United States. 5. Libraries—United States—Marketing. I. Title.
   Z678.6.L36 2008
   025.1'974—dc22   2008007425

ISBN-13: 978-0-8389-3575-0

Printed in the United States of America
12 11 10 09 08   5 4 3 2 1

Dedicated to my loyal staff and volunteers, whose efforts enabled our small public library to live long and prosper

CONTENTS

After a career in the technical publishing and computer industries, in 2002 I returned to my librarian roots and became director of a small public library in rural Lancaster County, Pennsylvania. I am the first full-time and first certified director in the library's forty-year history.

When I took the job, I expected it to be a genteel and relaxing position. I was wrong. Rather, it turned out to be the greatest and most fulfilling work challenge I have ever faced. In order to keep the public library financially viable, functionally relevant, and operationally efficient, I was forced to draw upon virtually all of my corporate experience in finance, marketing, public relations, and human relations, as well as my limited handyman's skills. I also required a lot of on-the-job training. I learned things that they do not teach either in the corporate world or in library school. I learned how to build, motivate, and rely upon a group of dedicated part-time staff and volunteers and a pro bono board of trustees. I learned how to identify and tap both conventional and unconventional sources of operating and development funds. I learned how to play small town politics. I learned how to work with the media to get the word out. Above all, I learned how to assess and respond to the needs of the various and diverse constituent communities that a public library serves. Most important, I learned how to earn and keep a community's loyalty, trust, and support.

My small library's board, staff, and I did what was required to get the job done with little homage to tradition or convention. Although it may be blasphemous for a librarian writing about libraries to say this, and I might not recommend this for every library, we broke with the traditional advice of library management texts (you might say we threw away the book) and did what we had to do in order to survive. In a time of economic and cultural challenges, our test was ensuring the continued ability of our public library to effectively respond to the lifelong learning needs of our community. Our mission was to satisfy as many as possible of our constituents' learning and information needs. We sought creative ways of doing more with very limited resources. When our government funding was cut, we found new ways of earning money.

To our surprise, we not only survived but we thrived. We began to earn local, regional, and even national recognition and awards. In February 2006 the Bill and Melinda Gates Foundation and *Library Journal* selected us as the "Best Small Library in America." To my further surprise, Laura Pelehach of the American Library Association then invited me to share with my colleagues what I have learned about ensuring a small public library's survival in the form of this book.

Every librarian secretly dreams of having a book of his own authorship sitting on his library's shelves. Therefore, I worked up my courage and accepted Laura's challenge to write this guide as a sort of cookbook for small public library survival. I hope my homemade recipes will work in your kitchen and help provide tasty and nutritious sustenance at your library's table to allow you to grow stronger.

Of course, not all these recipes will be suitable for every library. Readers will want to find those approaches that work best in their own situations, depending on the size of their libraries, their legal and tax bases, and so on. But it is my hope that readers will be able to apply at least some of the approaches from this book to their own situations in ways that are feasible and helpful. The ideas I suggest in this book have worked in my public library, which is structured as an independent 501(c)(3) not-for-profit corporation that receives only partial government support. Because only about 15 percent of U.S. public libraries are independent corporations, though, it might be wise for library officials to solicit the advice and consent of their library's governing body as well as its legal advisor and accountant prior to applying some of the unconventional techniques I propose.

CHAPTER ONE

WHY THIS BOOK IS NECESSARY

Most U.S. Public Libraries Are Small Public Libraries

The National Center for Education Statistics (NCES) tells us that in 2004 there were 9,207 public libraries in the United States.[1] Of these, 7,228 libraries, or 78.5 percent, were considered "small" libraries because they served areas with populations of 25,000 or less. There were twelve fewer small libraries reported in 2004 than the year before, prima facie evidence that small libraries are battling for their survival, and their number is declining.

If you believe, as I do, that the public library is the core institution for lifelong learning in America, then the small public library is the backbone of this institution. However, now more than ever before, the small public library is struggling for its very survival and may be considered to be under siege.

Small Public Libraries Are under Siege and Squeeze

The small public library is facing a number of major challenges. These include decreases in public funding, competition from the Internet and other electronic technologies, changing socioeconomic conditions, and learning and leisure activities that tend to deemphasize reading and library visits. We are being asked to prove our relevance in the face of fluid and often conflicting community needs and demographics. This was brought home to me when I returned to my librarian roots and became the director of a small public library in the Pennsylvania Dutch country after spending more than thirty years in the executive ranks of industry. I hired on to be the first full-time, certified director of a rural public library that had been run by part-time, nonprofessional employees and volunteers for nearly forty years. I took the job in the interest of devoting the remainder of my career to what I naively thought would be a form of relaxed and intellectual public service, removed from the preoccupation with making money that had dominated my prior thinking in the corporate world.

Little did I dream that I would end up spending about 50 percent of my time seeking the resources necessary to keep the library open while attempting to convince the community, government, educators, and foundations that the library was relevant, useful, and necessary, as well as a good investment.

My experience, alas, is not atypical among the directors of America's small public libraries. The concern about the future of small public libraries in America is great enough to cause the Bill and Melinda Gates Foundation to invest considerable money and effort in ensuring the sustainability of small and rural public libraries and their computer activities. Whether you call it *sustainability* or *survivability*, it is the battle that many small public libraries are fighting just to stay alive. A look at today's newspapers and library professional literature will yield such depressing headlines as "County Cuts Library Budget," "Libraries Struggling to Survive," "Funding Cuts Force Library Cutbacks," "Library Closures Result from Budget Cuts," and "Library Support Referendum Fails."

This situation has prompted librarian Ed D'Angelo to write a book on the siege of public libraries titled *Barbarians at the Gates of the Public Library* (2006). We face a troubling paradox, for while funding declines, library use and need seem to increase. The SirsiDynix chief statistician Robert E. Molyneux surveyed national public library trends from 1992 to 2003 and concluded: "Public libraries in the United States, in aggregate, have seen usage increase and revenues decline."[2]

At best, the American public library, and particularly the small public library, is suffering from benign neglect or, at worst, is under direct attack as an institution of learning and information. Why?

Direct Government Tax Support of Public Libraries Is Declining

Most small public libraries in the United States are fighting an ongoing battle to prove their relevance to funding agencies and find the resources to survive. We are faced with decreasing public funding and intense competition from a plethora of electronic information storage and dissemination media. Our traditional small town communities are experiencing rapid changes in demographics, employment, and economics. Small library boards, staff, and volunteers must devote increasing amounts of concern and effort to raising funds, garnering necessary community and government support, and attracting back patrons whose interest in libraries and reading may have lapsed.

The reasons for the national decline in public library support are manifold:

- growing taxpayer resistance to tax increases
- increased competition with other public services for limited government dollars
- increased competition from other information, learning, and entertainment providers
- population shifts and changing demographics leading to changes in library use patterns
- evolution from visual to oral communication (i.e., the move from reading to listening)

- questions regarding the value and relevance of the traditional public library in the twenty-first century's environment of instant electronic information delivery

In my five years as director of a small public library, I have had to face some unexpected and unprecedented funding challenges. My library has experienced a 43 percent cut in state public library aid, has battled against a proposed 20 percent cut in county library aid, and has watched county voters reject even a county tax referendum that would have provided a mere twenty-four dollars per family each year to ensure public library survival. Public libraries across the United States are facing similar threats to their hitherto stable government support. However, despite this ominous situation, I believe small public libraries can find the resources they require by becoming resourceful, innovative, and, when necessary, unconventional in seeking support and in being responsive to their community.

They can do so by employing the strategic market analysis, public relations, and planning techniques that have proven themselves in the business world. Why not use business tools in a library setting? Why not view our public libraries as business entities, albeit not-for-profit businesses, that serve the needs of specific communities, or "market customer bases"? We can respond to the needs of our defined "target" markets and use public relations tools to attract their attention and use. If satisfied, they will in turn support us, both economically and politically. We must not accept the assault against our public libraries passively, and we must defend and preserve these irreplaceable and uniquely American institutions.

How Can We Fight Back?

We are learning that if our libraries are to survive in the current environment, their leaders must begin to think and behave like savvy small-business CEOs and boards and learn to apply effective promotion and marketing strategies to win funding, patrons, and support. We have to adopt a new, positive, self-reliant and self-supporting model that emphasizes seeking and employing alternate asset sources when traditional government funding wanes. When we experience government funding cuts, we have to look at the "glass as half full" and identify new resources, develop new partnerships, and harvest additional community skills and assets. This differs from the old "glass half empty" deficiency model where libraries tend to focus on what's missing and look for ways to reduce services and cut costs when their government income declines.

In a hard practical sense, I have found that survival of the small public library depends on two *C* words: *communication* and *cash*. If you can effectively communicate with your community and maintain a flow of sufficient cash, you can survive and even flourish if you spend the cash wisely. That is what we did at my library.

In my first year as director, when I learned of the massive 43 percent cut in state public library aid, I chose not to go the route other nearby public libraries were going: 15 of the 17 libraries in my county cut back on hours, programs, and staff. I, though, could not capitulate. I was loath to give in and reduce my library's services and hours in my first six months as a director.

My initial fact-finding had indicated that the residents of the five municipalities served by my library had some real information and learning needs that were not being met by any other agencies. In my heart, I believed that my library could successfully address these needs if given sufficient financial, intellectual, and material resources. Rather than throw in the towel, I decided to apply some standard industry marketing and management techniques to generate and efficiently utilize the needed resources. A certain degree of desperation caused me to employ means that were unconventional (at least for libraries).

With the support of my board of trustees, staff, and volunteers, we beat the bushes for funds and donations in kind while formulating imaginative, albeit low-cost, programs in response to community needs. Corporate marketing experience had convinced me that modesty was a false virtue when seeking donations and patrons. I had learned during my years in corporate America that the media would readily print or broadcast your story if you put together well-written press releases in a style that attracts readers and requires minimal editing. We began to generate these press releases and they, in turn, yielded feature stories. The word began to spread that the library was a valuable community asset, worthy of public and private support which was immediately required.

Our use of proven industry public relations (PR) techniques generated increasing support and attracted more patrons as well as more patron diversity. A virtuous circle took shape. The local and county press began to regularly feature our programs, and a weekly newspaper even offered me a regular library column. Donations of money, hardware, and services began to flow in. More volunteers came forward. The favorable publicity helped us to write winning grant proposals, which yielded funds for new initiatives, which drew more patrons and visibility. In response to a positive press and popular library programs, organizations began to come forth to voluntarily offer us partnerships and grants. These organizations included foundations, service clubs, governments, labor unions, and even high school student groups.

Despite this apparent onslaught of goodwill, we did not sit back and rely only on the generosity of others. We also initiated a range of new income-generating activities to supplement our traditional Library Friends Annual Book Sale and Friends bookstore fund-raisers. New fund-raising activities included establishing a U.S. passport application acceptance agency in the library, an annual benefit auction, a parking-lot flea market, cartridge and cell phone recycling, and surplus book sales on the Internet. We rented out our meeting rooms to local businesses and community groups, and in one case we let a local computer instructor use our computer lab free in return for her teaching computer courses to library patrons. These fund-raising and fund conservation efforts proved successful. We were not only able to plug the money gap left by state funding cuts, but also earned enough extra cash to allow for expansion of our programs, our acquisitions, and our staff.

We were pleasantly surprised when our new programs began to win local, regional, and even national recognition and awards, the pinnacle being when *Library Journal* and the Bill and Melinda Gates Foundation named us the Best Small Library in America in 2006.

There may be critics who would question holding up my small public library as a model when we exhibit such a relatively low level of total support (less than eleven dollars per capita). I, too, truly wish that we could report a much higher per capita support level, but alas, that is not to be. To these critics I say that our experience shows that, regardless of its level of public support, a small library can still aspire to achieve excellence. By being resourceful and imaginatively finding alternative resources and conceiving low-overhead, high-quality programs, that library might just reach its goals. As they say, "If life gives you lemons, make some lemonade."

How Can This Book Help?

This book is not a scholarly treatise, nor will it advise on how to perform the daily operational tasks involved in running a small public library. There are already many other books from the ALA and others that fill this role. It is, instead, designed to guide small public library administrators in fighting the battle for sufficient support and recognition. It endeavors to provide a set of practical tools, guidelines, and strategies to help not only win the battle but to excel in providing library service. It is written to counsel librarians and trustees on the planning, promotion, and funding of a small public library using industry-based marketing and management techniques. It addresses the strategic tasks of planning, defining markets and user needs, designing relevant library services and products, finding needed resources, and carrying out effective promotion in a small public library context.

It is my observation that many who are charged with the responsibility of ensuring small public library sustainability lack marketing experience or training, perhaps because of the outmoded belief that public librarians do not require this skill. I learned essential marketing skills through thirty years in industry, not in library school. This book is, therefore, designed to give public library leaders, be they directors, trustees, volunteers, or Friends, a basic understanding of some of the more useful planning and marketing tools they can employ to ensure their library's survival and success.

This book's aim is to give a small public library's leadership the tools they need to do the following:

1. Define their community's library service needs.
2. Develop responsive programs.
3. Generate the resources necessary to support these programs.
4. Promote the library and its programs to patron and funding communities.

This is a practical guide written for the small library director and trustee. It addresses real issues that confront small public libraries. It provides tested strategies to allow libraries to respond to "threats" and turn them into "opportunities" for improving library services and status. It will guide them in defining, segmenting, and ranking their community's library needs and translating those needs into strategic plans and priorities. It will provide pointers for selling their plan to all stakeholders, including boards of directors, staff, government officials, funding and support agencies, and the public at large.

Real-world strategies will be presented for obtaining the resources needed to implement those plans, including money, materiel, services, and labor. Both conventional and unconventional resource generation will be evaluated, including municipal appropriations, grants, direct mail solicitation, gifts in kind, benefit events, and fee-based services. Techniques for developing beneficial partnerships with both public and private organizations will be explored. Ideas for developing low-cost but imaginative outside-of-the-box ideas for collection development, facilities management, and programming will be addressed. Alternative, economical sources for obtaining library commodities will be suggested. Techniques for effective low-cost marketing of the library and its offerings will be demonstrated, including promotion, media relations, and websites. Appendixes and bibliographies containing checklists, sample forms, and sources of additional information are also provided.

Of course, not all of the suggestions and tools found in these pages will be appropriate for every library. The structure of your library, how it is funded, how the board operates, and so on, will all have an effect on the strategies you employ to improve the standing of your library. Although small libraries across the country have many things in common, their differences will dictate which approaches are most suitable in your situation.

Regardless of these differences, though, a good place to start in formulating your library's survival plan is to define your library's role in the community, a topic covered in the next chapter.

NOTES

1. Adrienne Chute and others, *Public Libraries in the United States: Fiscal Year 2004* (Washington, DC: National Center for Education Statistics, 2006).
2. Robert E. Molyneux, "Recent Funding Trends," *American Libraries* 37, no. 3 (March 2006): 29.

CHAPTER TWO

DEFINING YOUR LIBRARY'S ROLE IN YOUR COMMUNITY

A Market-Oriented Approach

Getting Community Data via Conventional and Nonconventional Means

Industry marketing specialists know that a product or service will be successful only if it satisfies a need exhibited by a particular population, or what they call a *market segment*. The degree to which a market segment employs a particular product or service is termed *market penetration*. These simple guidelines can be key to ensuring that your library will be used, appreciated, and funded by the communities it serves. The target market segment population of a public library typically is the individual and corporate residents of a defined geographic region known as the library's service area. This area usually is assigned to the library by a government oversight agency. For a small public library, it might be one or more municipalities in a single county or a local school district.

In defining the needs of a particular library market segment, it is important to recognize that your target population has two basic sub-segments: (1) those who already use the library, and (2) those who do not (yet) use the library. It is much easier to define the characteristics and needs of current library users than those who are potential users. In the sections below we will discuss some tools you can use to identify both types.

Methods for Defining Current Patrons and Their Needs

There are five basic methods you can employ to segment your current patron base and define their library service needs:

1. Analysis of library cardholder data
2. Analysis of circulation statistics and reserve requests
3. Analysis of reference queries
4. Formal and informal surveys
   a. Questionnaires
   b. Formal interviews

      c.   Focus interviews

      d.   Focus groups

  5. Observation

Analysis of Library Cardholder Data

Most computer-based circulation systems will allow you to generate statistical reports from the data typically collected about cardholders. You can use these reports to generate cardholder statistics, which can be analyzed to give you relative demographics on your target audience, with breakdowns by such factors as age, gender, and geographic area of residence.

Analysis of Circulation Statistics and Reserve Requests

Modern computer-based circulation systems allow the librarian to collect and analyze generic information on which items are being borrowed and by what types of borrowers. To protect patron privacy, the linking of patron names with specific titles or classes of borrowed information is generally prohibited. The library planner will find these data useful in planning programs, acquisitions, and fund-raising. Analyzing relative circulation statistics by type of borrowed material such as genre, subject, and authors, plus the subject and direction of reference queries, can provide valuable insight on user interests and needs. Keeping track of titles that have built long waiting lists of reserves will provide a good indication of which subjects and authors are popular within your community. Some advanced circulation systems such as Millennium will even let you analyze library circulation figures by day of the week and time of day. Use these tools rather than speculation and you can determine more precisely who visits the library.

Analysis of Reference Queries

It can be useful to maintain a log of reference inquiries that can later be grouped by category and then studied to learn what research topics are of interest to your clientele. Your findings here will help you improve your collection and make it more valuable to your patrons. For example, a review of my library's reference queries over a six-month period showed that a number were concerned with alternative energy sources, particularly with the use of ethanol produced from agricultural products. Thus forewarned, we ordered several books on alternative energy, including ethanol production, and also developed a bibliography/search guide (which we call a "pathfinder") on the topic. Later that year, when a controversial proposal was put forth to build a large ethanol production plant in an adjacent town, we were well prepared to meet the flood of requests on the topic.

Formal and Informal Surveys

Surveys can be formal, with precisely designed questionnaires or forms and statistical validation; or they can be informal, with judgmental analysis and minimal paperwork. I will cover both techniques here. In addition, appendix B provides examples of both techniques.

If at all possible, get the advice of a survey specialist in designing your questionnaires and analyzing your findings in order to ensure valid and unbiased results. Many universities have data analysis institutes that may be able to offer your library assistance in this regard. Also, check with your library's bylaws to see if there are any restrictions on gathering data via surveys.

Questionnaires

An excellent way to learn what patrons want is to ask them directly. You can do this via formal written questionnaires or by individual or group interviews. Formal fill-in questionnaires (as opposed to interviewer questioning) are a traditional technique for gathering information from specific market segments and offer greater predictive statistical validity (albeit less flexibility) than informal techniques. Paper questionnaires now are giving way to online computer questionnaires using handy tools such as SurveyMonkey and Zoomerang, but the principles are the same.

A fill-in questionnaire's main advantage is that the respondent completes the questionnaire on her own, so an interviewer is not required. This technique is therefore less labor-intensive than an interview. The main disadvantage of voluntary fill-in/voluntary return questionnaires is a low response rate. Typically, questionnaires are handed out or mailed to a sampling or complete group of targeted respondents in the hope that enough will be returned to make the survey meaningful. In designing your survey and to ensure survey validity, try to get advice from a survey specialist or a statistician on market sample selection, optimum market segment sample sizes, and required levels of response. The specialist can also advise you on how to prepare unbiased questions and how to reduce and analyze survey results.

Survey questions can be formulated in four basic modes:

1. Narrative fill-in
2. Multiple-choice
3. Multiple-choice ranking
4. Yes/no

You can mix or match these types of questions. A broad narrative question gives the most latitude to the respondent, but it is the most difficult to fill in and to analyze, and needed data may be left out. Multiple-choice and yes/no questions give more survey control, but require many more questions to elicit exactly the kind of information you're looking for. However, all types of questions can get you the information you require, as the example below demonstrates.

Narrative Question Example

Indicate what type of books you like to read in the box below:

```
┌─────────────────────────────────────────────────────────────┐
│                                                             │
│                                                             │
│                                                             │
└─────────────────────────────────────────────────────────────┘
```

Multiple-Choice Question Example

Check the type of book(s) you like to read:

- ❏ Fiction
- ❏ Travel
- ❏ Biography
- ❏ History
- ❏ Do-It-Yourself
- ❏ Other (specify) _____

Multiple-Choice Ranking Question Example

Rank these types of books by preference (1 = most preferred; 5 = least preferred):

- ❏ Fiction
- ❏ Travel
- ❏ Biography
- ❏ History
- ❏ Do-It-Yourself
- ❏ Other (specify) _____

Yes/No Question Example

Do you like to read fiction?

❏ Yes ❏ No

Do you like travel books?

❏ Yes ❏ No

Critical Incident Question Example

When did you last visit the library? _____

What information did you look for? _____

Did you find what you wanted? _____

Were you happy with your visit?

❏ Yes ❏ No

Why? _____

Formal Interviews

In formal interviews, a questionnaire that is similar to the formal respondent-completed questionnaire cited above is employed. However, in this case the interviewer poses the questions to the respondent and records the responses, usually on a one-on-one basis. When performed by an objective interviewer, this type of survey can yield excellent results, but it is very labor-intensive and requires skilled interviewers.

Focus Interviews

I personally prefer interviews using focus interview or focus group techniques, which I successfully employed for years in industry.

Focus interviewing is a relatively informal mode of data-gathering using broad-based questions posed by an interviewer who is skilled in the technique. Although the interviewer starts with a set of prepared questions, he or she is free to expand upon these and follow any new information paths that may seem promising. The principle behind focus interviewing is the same as that behind the focus group market and opinion survey technique, which is widely employed in marketing and political voter analysis.

Focus interviewing can be done either one-on-one or en masse as a focus group. The principles and outcomes are the same, but you get more depth in the one-on-ones. Start with a few broad-based questions such as the following:

"What are your most important information and educational needs?"

"Are your needs being met?"

"What do you like (or dislike) about the library?"

"What services would you like the library to introduce?"

"How would you feel about an XXX service?"

Then pick up and focus on relevant aspects of the individual's or group's answers and ask them to elaborate or explain, maintaining a dialogue until you get the depth of information you need. For example:

"You said that the library does not seem 'child friendly.' Can you tell me why you feel that way?"

"You feel the library should have more 'chick lit.' Can you elaborate?"

"Why do you borrow a lot of audio books?"

Because this technique is somewhat unstructured, you might uncover some unexpected but useful information threads as you delve into various areas. For example, our library's collection of large-print books was rarely used, and we were questioning its value. However, when we conducted focused interviews with homebound members of our community, we discovered that most had vision limitations and had a great need for these large-print books. The reason they did not borrow them was because their handicaps prevented them from physically visiting the library. Using this new knowledge, we obtained a Library Services and Technology Act (LSTA) grant to start a "Reads on Wheels" book-delivery service to the homebound and nursing homes. As a result, our circulation of large-print editions skyrocketed and we had to borrow additional titles from neighboring libraries via interlibrary loan.

Focus Groups

In the focus group technique, a group of about five to ten individuals who represent a specific community segment (e.g., young mothers, senior citizens, business people, etc.) are presented with some leading questions or statements. They are asked to respond to these, and a group facilitator or interviewer will develop certain threads in the responses in order to obtain useful feedback information. One strength of focus group interviewing is that the members of the group interact with each other as well as with the interviewer. However, a skilled interviewer is needed to keep the discussions on target and to discourage strong-minded individuals from dominating the interaction.

If you are surveying communities in which some residents may not be proficient in English, it can be very useful (and demonstrate the library's sensitivity) to translate your surveys into the target group's language and to use interviewers with foreign language skills. In addition, consider encouraging key staff to learn or improve their foreign language skills by taking language courses or by self-instruction. Knowing a foreign language is a growing need, and my home state initiated a series of courses on Occupational Spanish for Library Personnel in 2006. Several of my library's staff and I were among the first to sign up for this instruction. As a result, I can now greet our Spanish-speaking patrons by saying, "Buenos días. Mi nombre es Herb. Yo soy el bibliotecario. ¿En qué le puedo ayudar?"

Observation

Leave your office and walk around the library to learn how it is being used. A popular management book of 1982, *In Search of Excellence: Lessons from America's Best-Run Companies*, by Thomas J. Peters and Robert H. Waterman, coined the phrase *management by walking around*. The authors advised the manager to leave his office and regularly walk around and observe his operations. This advice also applies to libraries and librarians. Roam your library and unobtrusively observe how patrons interact with your collections, your staff, your facilities, and each other. You will learn a lot and you will likely find that patrons stop you to volunteer advice, ask questions, and even thank you for serving their library needs. Get into the habit of making regular "rounds" and spending time at the circulation desk. I have gotten some of my best ideas, such as computer courses for seniors and lending computers, by just walking around and talking to patrons. It also is good PR for people to see that their library director is accessible and interested in their opinions. This also applies to reference librarians.

I know of some libraries that have instituted "roving reference" where reference librarians walk around wearing a tag reading "How can I help you?"

Determining Patron Needs Is a Continuing Activity

Your data-gathering by market segment should be an ongoing process. Interact often with your patrons and community members and ask their opinions. Your queries do not have to be formal. For example, when members of our staff make homebound deliveries, they routinely ask assisted-living facility residents and staff about their library needs and satisfaction levels. By doing this they learn new things not taught in library school. For example, a nursing home activities director taught us that cognitively impaired individuals (such as Alzheimer's victims) enjoy large-format picture books and nonviolent children's films. In another assisted-living facility, a resident who is a retired teacher asked us to deliver children's panel books and basic reading primers so she could teach illiterate fellow residents how to read.

When gathering data about patrons and their information needs, it is very important to protect their rights of privacy. Collecting aggregate data by market segment group is fine, but we should neither maintain nor report on the information-use habits of specific individuals.

Defining Non-users and Their Needs via Population Demographics and Market Segmentation

Identifying non-users and their potential library needs is difficult and requires some ingenuity and unconventional techniques. First we need to define the demographics of the community at large and then their learning and recreational needs.

Defining the Demographics of the Community You Serve

In the previous section, we discussed how you could analyze library patron data to get useful demographic statistics on library users, such as age and gender distribution, towns of residence, and so on. You will need to collect these types of data—and then some—to determine how your library can best reach out to your entire community, including those who do not currently employ library services. To determine how to draw non-users to the library, you should try to determine their interests, educational levels, English proficiency, computer ability, and library awareness levels.

The overall community data you seek should include the following:

1. Socioeconomic factors
   a. Income
   b. Education
   c. Computer literacy

2. Ethnicity/English capability

3. Special populations

4. Age levels

5. Literacy

6. Library's current "market penetration" (or "market share") for each market segment

7. Population's physical locations and political units

8. Current and potential means of access to the library

9. Media channels employed (e.g., newspapers read, electronic media channels, etc.)

There are several national and local sources that can provide you with demographic and socioeconomic data for the specific ZIP codes your library serves. These include U.S. Census data available via the U.S. Census website (www.census.gov), regional development authority statistics for your area, university urban and regional data institutes, local municipalities and school districts, and commercial demographic database services such as SRC/Demographics Now in California. Most of these services will provide the data you require pro bono if you tell them you are a not-for-profit public library.

Here is an example of how these data can be helpful in defining an area's demographics. I observed an apparent change in the ethnic makeup of the area served by my library but needed to verify this before factoring it into our strategic planning. I was able to obtain a compilation of comparative area population ethnicity data for the period 2000–2005 collectively from the U.S. Census, Penn State University's Regional and Urban Studies Center, and SRC/Demographics Now. These data showed that the Latino population of my library's five-town service area had increased by more than 500 percent during the prior five-year time period. In another study, U.S. Census data showed that our area had a significant seniors population that included more than 1,000 homebound residents. These findings prompted us to revise our acquisitions, services, programs, and grant-seeking efforts to allow us to be more responsive to these two groups as their numbers increase.

Identifying and Prioritizing Community Information and Education Needs

For each targeted market segment you identify in your community, you will have to establish a relative priority as well as deciding which of its information and education needs your library will endeavor to satisfy. A small library with limited resources cannot fulfill every need of every potential patron, so a priority ranking of users and their needs is required.

After much soul-searching, my library adopted a relatively simple solution to this problem. We give top priority to those patrons whose learning needs are not addressed by any other community agency. In our case, the two top-priority groups that came out of this analysis were at opposite ends of the patron age spectrum. They were the preschoolers and seniors. Discussions with community leaders and library patrons and analysis of community resource directories told us that there were no nonsectarian preschool or senior centers or discrete educational programs for either of these groups in our service area. While not ignoring other market segments (e.g., working adults, teens, etc.), we did skew our programs, acquisitions, and publicity toward these two priority groups. They responded with record program attendance, increased library visits and circulation, and increased library support (both as cash and volunteers). The new services for seniors we conceived as a result of this analysis (i.e., homebound delivery, computer courses, laptop lending, and a Baby Boomers program series) enabled us to win both a $47,000 LSTA grant and the AARP's Award of Excellence for Library Services for Older Adults in 2005 and 2006.

Employing Community Information Resources

Some effective ways of defining the lifelong learning needs of your community include the following:

1. Analysis of local news media
2. Attendance at group meetings (e.g., service clubs, community service groups, social service agencies, etc.)
3. Surveying "typical" representatives
4. Surveying community leaders

This process of identifying and milking sources of information about your community will also serve you well when you disseminate information about your library to the community. Each input channel can serve as an output channel (see chapter 8 on marketing).

Analyzing Local News Media

You can learn a lot about what is going on in your community from the media. Check the community events and "local" sections of the major daily newspapers to learn about the focus of your community's interests and who the leaders and philanthropists are. Your weekly local merchandiser and penny-saver freebie papers can also provide a wealth of local information, because they publish virtually any local notices they receive as space fillers. Even the classified ads and auction notices can provide insight on which specific causes are being supported by local church and volunteer groups via flea markets, bazaars, and benefit auctions. Public service announcements and community bulletin boards aired by local public and commercial radio and TV stations and the cable services are also useful in this regard. Again, remember that these media will also broadcast news about your library that you may provide to them (see chapter 8).

Attending Group Meetings

The public library is not alone in seeking to serve the lifelong learning needs of the community. There are various other private and public organizations that also address aspects of this problem, although none, I believe, has as broad a scope as the public library. These organizations can include service clubs, community service groups, literacy advocacy organizations, social service agencies, school parent-teacher associations, church groups, and business associations. Try to identify the organizations whose missions are closest to those of your library. For example, the Literacy Councils and Kiwanis Clubs support literacy and, by extension, libraries. Selectively attend the open meetings of these groups, listen to and talk with their leaders, and learn which of their community needs fit in with your library's mission. When you visit these groups and attend their meetings, it is important to let them know who you are and that you are there because you want to learn how your library can partner with them to better serve the community. By doing this, you will get the word out about your library and demonstrate its positive public service attitude. You are sowing seeds that will yield future support.

Surveying "Typical" Representatives

Survey statisticians employ a technique they call "purposive" or "judgmental" sampling. This is based on the same premise behind the popular focus group method of market research. You can employ this technique in defining library needs. This practice requires that you first identify a target group (or "market segment") of real or potential library users whose needs you want to assess. Then you identify "typical" representatives of this market segment (i.e., those who most closely match the typical demographics and characteristics of the group). You then query these "stereotypes" to determine their needs, interests, and expectations regarding your library, which you then extrapolate into the needs of the group as a whole. You can gather the information from the stereotype either via the focus interview mode or by a more formal written or oral survey questionnaire. However, a word of caution is necessary here. If the results are to be accurate, the selection of the "sample" interviewees and the interview questions must be objective and free of any biases. A skilled, unbiased interviewer can derive excellent insight into the learning habits and needs of a market segment and what your library can do to serve that group. In these interviews, the interviewer must be courteous and respectful in questioning, and he must listen well to answers and exercise accuracy in recording responses. Keep the dialogue upbeat and you can make some good library friends along the way.

Surveying Community Leaders

Do not be hesitant about approaching your community leaders to seek their suggestions and guidance on library service priorities. Early in my career when I first started doing market research surveys, I felt reluctant to ask strangers for their opinions. An old hand mentored me by saying that virtually everyone loves to be considered an "expert" and feels flattered when someone asks for their advice and help on a problem.

Drawing on this advice from my past, I found that I could approach virtually any community leader, such as a mayor, town manager, municipal council member, school superintendent, labor union leader, chamber of commerce director, clergyman, or newspaper editor, to ask for help and advice in defining the "community's library needs" and get a very positive reception. As both thought leaders and sounding boards for their constituents, these people will usually be quite happy to give you advice on both community needs and on the realpolitik of gaining community support and funding.

For example, as a brand-new public library director, I visited the borough manager of one of the five municipalities served by my library to both pay my respects and to solicit advice. He readily suggested which community residents he thought needed our services most and gave me excellent advice on how to best approach the town councils to request library appropriations. He even offered to supply the library with such municipal support services as trash collection, water, sewer, and parking lot marking on a pro bono basis. As a quid pro quo, I offered to let the borough use our conference rooms for police training and town meetings and to sell municipal trash collection permits at our circulation desk. This became the foundation of a strong working partnership, which continues to yield both excellent advice and municipal support for the library.

Identifying and Evaluating Your "Competition" in the Community

The gist of this section could be summed up as "if you ain't the only game in town and you can't beat 'em, then join 'em" (or at least borrow their best ideas).

There are a variety of channels beyond your public library by which your current and potential patrons can pursue their educational, informational, and recreational needs. In marketing terms, your market penetration and market share will never be 100 percent. "Competing" information providers include public broadcast and print media, the Internet, the educational establishment, movies, sports, scouts groups, churches, clubs, community centers, video stores, bookstores, and even other libraries. It will be a waste of your library's limited resources to attempt to aggressively compete with all these other activities for patron attention. Instead, view your role as complementing them. Co-opt them when you can and emulate their best practices where feasible. Libraries actually already do this by offering access to the Internet, newspapers, and magazines.

For example, rather than compete with the local high school library, you can support them by sharing your surplus reading materials and asking them, in turn, to help you sign up high school students for public library cards. You can integrate local public and private school syllabi with your collections by identifying the reading materials relevant to homework assignments or projects so students can easily locate and employ them. You can offer "homework helper" support to students. At my library, the close relationship we have with the local school library is demonstrated by the fact that several high school library staff members serve on our public library volunteer team.

Instead of banning iPods, PDAs, Blackberries, and the portable computers that are so popular with young people, enable them by making your library a WiFi hot spot. Feature the library as a global network gateway and encourage patrons to bring their communication devices into the library. Allow the scouts, soccer teams, and clubs to use your community rooms for their meetings. Visit your local video shops and bookstores and explore modes of cooperation with them. At our library, for example, Barnes and Noble Booksellers allows our volunteers to run their gift-wrapping stations during the holidays and lets us keep the wrapping fees earned. They also offer tax-exempt deep discounts on books purchased by us. The benefits derived from our visits to local video shops include our decision to adapt their user-friendly video arrangement system to our collections and their donation of surplus DVD cases to our library.

Libraries can learn from bookstores and can adapt and adopt their best practices. Our focus group interviews told us that one standard feature of major bookstores that readers loved was the café, which allowed them to sip a latte while browsing the books. Following this lead, public libraries are opening on-premises coffee shops and are finding them to be both popular and financially rewarding. (An insightful article on this by Chris Rippel of the Central Kansas Library System is titled "What Libraries Can Learn from Bookstores" and is available online via WebJunction. See http://www.ckls.org/~crippel/marketing/bookstore.html.)

Seek partnerships and promote idea-sharing relationships with other public libraries. Rather than competing with the public libraries in adjacent towns, why not develop a common patron database, honor each other's library cards, and coordinate service hours to allow for sharing of patrons and reduced duplication of effort? You and your patrons will all benefit. Share ideas about new sources of income generation with other libraries. We were the first public library in our county to accept the U.S. State Department's invitation to become a passport application acceptance agency. Not only did this new service draw new people into the library, but it also yielded more than $25,000 per year in fees. When we shared the news of the significant income and community goodwill we derived from this service with our peer libraries, four other county libraries also decided to become passport agencies, and one of these libraries now earns $100,000 per year in passport fees. In return, this library advised us on how to set up a passport photo service that now yields us an additional $5,000 in annual income. A fringe benefit of something like a passport agency in a library is that it brings in new faces. We find that about 50 percent of the passport applicants who visit our library do not hold library cards, so we offer them membership and almost all accept.

Once you have a clear picture of your community's demographics and needs relevant to your library, you can begin to address the development of your strategic plan. The next chapter will show you how to do this.

CHAPTER THREE

TRANSLATING COMMUNITY NEEDS
INTO A STRATEGIC PLAN

Overview of the Strategic Planning Process

Strategic planning is a common long-range planning practice found in both industry and the not-for-profit sector. It is a technique borrowed from the military that can be readily adapted to the public library. To demonstrate, a typical military strategic plan hierarchy might look like this:

Mission: Win the war

Goal: Conquer the Pacific theater from east to west

Objective: Take the area island by island (Guadalcanal, Iwo Jima, etc.)

Strategy: Take Iwo Jima and set up airfield there by August 1

Tactics: Air and naval bombardment followed by amphibious landing

Tasks:

1. Assemble, equip, and train a task force by June 1

    Three Marine and one Army division

    A fleet of 300 ships

    Five aircraft squadrons

    100 landing craft

2. Commence naval and air bombardment on June 1

3. Mount amphibious invasion on June 8, and so on

A strategic plan is a document that gives your library a structured, hierarchical, and sequential method to define where it wants to go and then what strategies it can use to get there. There is no predefined size for a strategic planning document. It could be 10 or 100 pages. Make it only large enough to cover all of the goals and objectives you need to address. It should be written in a language that your library's board and staff can understand and act upon. Do not create an overly technical strategic plan for your board if they are primarily laypeople who might have difficulty understanding library jargon.

There are scores of books on strategic planning that offer a variety of different definitions of the process. However, here is a simple functional definition of the strategic planning process and its steps that has worked for me over the years:

1. Define your organization's mission.
2. Define long- and short-range goals toward achieving your mission.
3. Define specific quantitative and scheduling objectives on the way to achieving your goals.
4. Define strategies and tactics necessary to achieve your objectives.
5. Define resources and timetable required to meet each objective.

Each of these steps is treated in detail below.

Your strategic plan document can be a valuable guide to your library's management and development. It can perform dual service, serving both as the library's road map to give you direction and as a gauge against which you can measure your progress and results. It also allows you to validate and explain your library's purpose and scope to your funding agencies and constituents. In fact, many funding or granting bodies now request that you validate your grant request by cross-referencing its scope and purpose to the appropriate cited sections of your strategic long-range plan.

Developing Your Statement of Mission

The first step in developing a strategic plan is a statement of mission for your library. In strategic planning, all efforts must be in support of the organization's mission. Indeed, if your library is a not-for-profit IRS category 501(c)(3) tax-exempt entity, your mission statement must specify your public service role, and both the federal and state governments have the right to audit your activities and validate them against your official statement of mission to determine if you should be taxed or not. If yours is an independent library, a mission and purpose statement should be part of your articles of incorporation or constitution and bylaws. If yours is a branch of a larger library system, then refer back to the parent organization's statement of mission as this will also be yours, although you may want to translate and refine it down to your local level (with your system's approval, of course). If you do not have a mission statement, or if you are not happy with the one you have, then work with your board or governing body to develop one that truly reflects the library's purpose and scope in your community. Whatever you do, be sure it is in keeping with the bylaws, guidelines, rules, and regulations governing your library. It's probably a good idea to check with your library's attorneys or other legal advisors to make sure you are following all applicable rules and regulations.

A mission statement can be as simple as "serving as the public library of the XXX community." It can be functional, such as "maintaining collections of books, periodicals, and audiovisual materials to consult and borrow; providing reference services; and conducting educational programs for the residents of XXX." It could be a bit lofty, such as "serving the lifelong learning needs of the XXX community," or it could be a combination of all of these approaches. Although your mission statement should accurately define your library's broad purpose and scope, avoid making it overly precise or media-specific, because this can hamper your library's evolution. For example, I once managed a century-old not-for-profit publishing company. When the organization began to publish digital-format editions online, as CD-ROMs, and in digital tape formats, the IRS initiated a tax audit of our activities. It challenged our tax-exempt status under the premise that by producing electronic products we had violated our 100-year-old mission statement, which referred only to paper book and periodical products. We eventually won the battle, but only after a lot of hard argument to convince the "revenuers" that publishing was content-centered, not medium-centered, and that a "book" is a "book" whether it is on paper or on a CD. Therefore, do not lock your library into specific activities and media, because you need a certain degree of flexibility so you can respond to inevitable future changes in patron needs and technologies. A well-written, service-oriented mission statement should remain valid despite changes in community demographics and in publishing and information-delivery technologies.

As a library director or trustee, try to spend a little bit of time thinking about your institution's raison d'être. Perhaps because I came into the role of a small town public librarian later in life, I find myself doing a lot of soul-searching on both the purpose of the public library in today's society and the role of my small library in its rural community. One thing that helped me to formulate my views on the library's role was a book edited by Ray Oldenburg titled *Celebrating the Third Place: Inspiring Stories about the "Great Good Places" at the Heart of Our Communities* (2002).

This book tells us that almost everybody has two places. They have their home and then they have their job (or school). The problem is that both of these places come with some built-in tensions, conflicts, and emotional baggage. Therefore, everyone needs a third place as a refuge where they feel comfortable, welcome, and relaxed. Oldenburg identifies third places, or "great good places," as neutral ground where people can gather and interact. In contrast to first places (home) and second places (work), third places allow people to put aside their concerns and simply enjoy the company, conversation, and ambience around them. Third places "host the regular, voluntary, informal, and happily anticipated gatherings of individuals beyond the realms of home and work." Oldenburg suggests that beer gardens, main streets, pubs, cafés, post offices, and other third places are the heart of a community's social vitality and the foundation of a functioning democracy. They promote social equality by leveling the status of guests, provide a setting for grassroots politics, create habits of public association, and offer psychological support to individuals and communities. When I read this, I asked myself, "Why not also offer the public library as a community's 'third place'?"

I sought to employ the concept of community ownership of the library in defining our place and mission, and I try to instill this attitude in our staff. I suggest to them that it's not their library that they are letting the public use. Instead, it's the community's library that we are being paid to manage. Therefore, we must be responsive to our patrons' needs and make them welcome. There was a time when the library staff viewed neighborhood latchkey kids who would hang around the library as unwelcome trespassers. Now we offer them the library as their "third place" and we even "deputize" some of them as library volunteers, giving them odd jobs to perform around the library. I can think of worse places for kids to hang out than in a public library. For some of these at-risk youth, exposure to the relatively wholesome library environment may balance the negative influences they can encounter on the streets or at home.

I have also noted with interest in the recent literature that some small public libraries across the country have started referring to themselves as the "community's living room." To take this concept one step further, a recent *New York Times* article suggested physically linking the home and the library by constructing urban buildings with a public library on the ground floor and apartments above it.[1]

To continue on the synthesis of your strategic plan, you next have to translate your mission statement into specific goals.

Defining Long- and Short-Range Goals

With your library's mission firmly in mind, digest the demographic data you have gathered on your library's current (and potential) patrons and their library needs and translate these into specific task-oriented library service goals. Goals can be long-term (i.e., two to five years) or short-term (i.e., immediate to two years) and can be somewhat conceptual, with or without specific, quantifiable end results and dates. Goals can incorporate both conventional and nonconventional library services and can even specify new community roles for the library. However, you should group your goals by four relevant and intersecting functional categories. By "intersecting" I mean that each goal will support and even eventually merge with other goals. For example, a services goal is virtually meaningless unless it is linked to a patron market segment goal.

It is a good idea to develop your strategic plan's goals by library administrative and operational category. Some suggested goal categories are as follows:

1. Administrative Goals
    a. Governance
    b. Facilities
    c. Funding
    d. Staffing
2. Services Goals
    a. Collections
    b. Programs/events
    c. Reference
    d. Circulation
3. Goals by Patron Market Segment
    a. Preschoolers
    b. Toddlers

   c.   Children

   d.   Youth and teens

   e.   Adults

   f.   Seniors

   g.   Specific ethnic groups

   h.   Handicapped

   i.   Business

   j.   Not for profit

4.   Community Relations Goals

   a.   Media relations

   b.   Advertising

   c.   Writing and publishing

   d.   Speaking

   e.   Attending meetings

   f.   Partnering

Each broad goal category and its cluster of more specific goals will logically intersect with and support one or more other categories and their goals. For example, if your library's service area has experienced an influx of Latinos, then you may want to establish the following strategic planning goals in response (with appropriate goal category indicated):

Broad Goal: To increase library awareness, use, and support in the Latino community (Patron Market Segment)

Specific Goals

- to identify and meet with Latino community leaders to determine and classify their community's needs and to increase their awareness of library services (Community Relations/Attending meetings)
- to establish Latino representation on the library board (Administrative/Governance)
- to obtain grant monies to expand services to the Latino market segment (Administrative/Funding)
- to hire new and/or train current staff members to provide Spanish-language capability in the library (Administrative/Staffing)
- to create bilingual patron finding aids, posters, and brochures (Services/Community Relations)
- to acquire Spanish-language and English as a Second Language (ESL) materials for the collections (Services/Collections)

- to develop after-school programs for Latino teens (Patron Market Segment/Services/Programs)
- to attract patrons by publicizing library services in Latino-oriented media (Community Relations/Media relations)

In the example above, note that Community Relations goals are found throughout the process. If the public library's raison d'être is to serve its community, then effective community relations are necessary to get the message to those whom you want to serve, your target market segments. Therefore, it is important that public libraries recognize Community Relations as a specific strategic goal area to be addressed and funded in their strategic plans. To do so effectively, library management must maintain open, bi-directional communication channels to all segments of the community. The input channels provide information to keep the library aware of its target community's changing demographics and learning needs, and the output channels keep the community aware of what the library is doing to satisfy the community's needs. You should recognize public relations as a discrete strategic goal area to ensure it will get the attention and resources it deserves. Marketing your library to its constituency is necessary for the library's survival and development. Even the very best library services have no value if they are not used.

You can develop a really comprehensive set of goals by working your way through the complete spectrum of the community's defined population market segments, developed as described above, and developing a set of services and outreach goals for each market segment.

Once you have developed a reasonably comprehensive set of strategic goals, assign priorities to them. Note that you don't have to initially develop a complete set of goals for your library. Instead, concentrate on developing first the set of goals needed to address your most immediate and important service needs that can be accomplished within a reasonable period of time (i.e., one to three years). In this rapidly changing world, strategic planning for operational objectives much beyond three years can be a waste of time. Certain goals, however, such as those involving major capital fundraising and construction efforts, may require longer-range projections of up to five years or more.

Next, develop basic criteria to prioritize your goals. Library priorities should reflect user priorities. Give higher priority to goals that address services to those patron groups that need the library most, such as

1. People whose needs are not satisfied by any other community institution
2. People whose needs are critical to those persons' quality of life
3. Patron needs where solutions provided by others involve costs beyond the average patron's financial resources
4. Critical services which yield the most benefit per library dollar

Now you can translate your defined and priority-ranked goals into a set of objectives.

Quantitatively Defining Specific Objectives to Achieve Your Goals

You will need to break down your goals into specific objective steps toward achieving them. Start at the beginning by sequentially listing each step necessary to get you from where you are to the desired result. Assign specific completion dates to each objective.

For example, we can take the first goal from the example above and break it down into specific objectives:

> Goal: Meet with Latino community leaders to define and classify their community's needs and to increase their awareness of library services
>
> Objective 1: Identify five to ten representative Latino community leaders
>> Elapsed time: two weeks
>> Completion date: June 1
>
> Objective 2: Schedule meetings with identified Latino leaders
>> Elapsed time: one week
>> Completion date: June 8
>
> Objective 3: Interview Latino leaders
>> Elapsed time: two weeks
>> Completion date: June 22
>
> Objective 4: Produce draft report of Latino community library needs
>> Elapsed time: three weeks
>> Completion date: July 13
>
> Objective 5: Review draft report with Latino community leaders and validate findings
>> Elapsed time: two weeks
>> Completion date: July 27
>
> Objective 6: Prepare and issue final report on Latino community needs
>> Elapsetd time: two weeks
>> Completion date: August 10
>
> Total elapsed time to achieve goal: twelve weeks

By breaking each of your goals down into achievable objectives, assigning an elapsed time to each objective, and then adding the elapsed times, you can get an initial timetable for implementing your strategic plan. Keep the timetable flexible and modify it if required by changing circumstances.

Defining Strategies and Tactics to Achieve Your Objectives

Here is where you get down to planning the specific details of your battle tactics. For each objective you have defined, under each goal you will develop the approach which you plan to take to achieve the objective. Just like in a real military battle, you may conceive a preferred approach and also a secondary (or even tertiary) fallback approach in case the first (or second) one does not succeed. What you will do, essentially, is to think out, step-by-step, how you will sequentially perform the steps necessary to reach the objective. (Make sure you keep your library board, other officials, and staff apprised of your progress while defining the strategies and tactics you plan to use to achieve your objectives.)

Using the same objectives from the example above, the development of strategies might look like this:

Goal: Meet with Latino community leaders to define and classify their community's needs and to increase their awareness of library services

Objective 1: Identify five to ten representative Latino community leaders

    Strategy: Search media and ask local institutions and patrons

    Tactics and tasks:

        Search local media

        Search Internet

        Search directories, Yellow Pages

        Contact Latino churches, clubs, and so on

        Confer with representative library patrons

    Elapsed time: two weeks

    Completion date: June 1

Objective 2: Schedule meetings with Latino leaders

    Strategy: Focus meeting approach

    Tactics and tasks:

        Alt. 1: Invite leaders as a group to a focus discussion at the library

        Alt. 2: Set up individual focus interviews

    Elapsed time: one week

    Completion date: June 8

Objective 3: Interview Latino leaders

    Strategy: Conduct focus interviews

    Tactics and tasks:

        Alt. 1: Conduct focus group session

        Alt. 2: Conduct individual focus interviews

    Elapsed time: two weeks

    Completion date: June 22

Objective 4: Produce report of Latino community library needs

    Strategy: Prepare draft report for review

    Tactics and tasks:

        Compile interview results

        Develop findings

        Prepare draft report

    Elapsed time: three weeks

    Completion date: July 13

Objective 5: Review draft report with Latino community leaders and validate findings

    Strategy: Validate draft report

    Tactics and tasks:

        Distribute draft report to Latino community leaders

        Alt. 1: Invite them all to a group discussion at the library

        Alt. 2: Meet with them individually

    Elapsed time: two weeks

        Completion date: July 27

Objective 6: Prepare and issue final report on Latino community needs

    Strategy: Disseminate report

    Tactics and tasks:

        Revise report as necessary

        Issue final report on Latino community library needs

    Elapsed time: two weeks

    Completion date: August 10

Total elapsed time to achieve goal: twelve weeks

Follow-Up Objective 7: Implement Latino patron service plan

    Strategy: Obtain grant

    Tactics and tasks:

        Develop implementation plan to satisfy needs

        Identify grant agency

        Write grant request to obtain resources

        Allocate resources to implement plan

        Review results against needs

        Make modifications as necessary

Elapsed time: To be determined based on findings of needs study

Completion date: To be determined

Every strategic plan task will require some outlay of resources, which also will need to be defined in your strategic plan.

Defining Resources and Timetables for Each Objective

Once you have laid out each strategic and tactical step necessary to achieve each objective with its estimated timetable, you can calculate the resources you will need to actually perform and conclude the work. In general, you will need four types of resources to complete each strategic task and achieve your objectives and goals: cash, labor, materiel, and facilities.

For each objective and then for each goal, you can calculate the necessary resources by category. Add the objective resources up and you then have the total cost for implementing your strategic plan. Structure your objectives to reflect library products and services categories (e.g., collection objectives, circulation objectives, reference objectives, program objectives). You can then compile and project the costs of each category of products or services. If you convert your labor, materiel, and facilities needs into the cash cost necessary for the acquisition of each item or service (or "dollarize" them, as they say in industry), you then get the total cost stated as a cash common denominator. Add up all the elapsed times, overlapping those that can be done in parallel, and you then get the total time required to implement your strategic plan. You will then have your plan's total of goals, costs, and elapsed schedule time in one strategic long-range plan package—a road map to your library's future.

A good strategic plan is a living document to be followed but that is also to be continually revised and updated to reflect changing needs and resources. The people involved in your library's administration and operation should be made aware of the library's strategic plan and of any changes to it.

Obtaining Support for Your Library's Strategic Plan

Before you begin to implement your strategic plan, you must ensure that all those who will share in its implementation understand and support it. This is especially true of your library's governing body and management team.

In an ideal library environment, the trustees and professional staff will all have participated in the development of the strategic plan and will therefore understand and support its goals and objectives. This is important no matter who writes the plan, whether it is the library director, the trustees, or a consultant. Every decision maker should sign off on it. Provide all key players not familiar with the plan with copies, including executive summaries, and meet with them to solicit comments, questions, and even objections. Act decisively and honestly to resolve any negative feelings or conflicts about the plan prior to its implementation. Once the trustees and senior staff are comfortable with the strategic plan, vet it with your junior and clerical staff, library volunteers, and library Friends group. A good plan can stand up under scrutiny, and this sharing of goals will ensure the continued support of those your library depends upon.

Make sure that your strategic plan is in compliance with all of the compacts, statutes, or rules that govern your library. If you are receiving endowment funds from a foundation or an estate, your strategic plan should not conflict with any provisions of the gift agreement. Before the strategic plan is promulgated, you must also verify that nothing in it is in violation of any provisions of your state's library code, federal library funding guidelines (e.g., E-Rate, Children's Internet Protection Act), or federal IRS 501(c)(3) or state tax-exempt rules. Be sure to touch base with your library's legal and tax advisors as necessary during all phases of strategic planning.

A good strategic plan can prove valuable as your library pursues various sources of funds and resources. For example, it is not unusual for a foundation or government granting agency to request the specific section of your long-range plan that relates to a grant application. An official, board-approved strategic plan legitimizes any library activities done in accord with it and helps defend against potential challenges. In addition, if a critic challenges a particular library activity, it helps to cite the section of the board-approved strategic plan in which the issue is covered.

Once your strategic plan is completed, consider sending copies of the plan or its executive summary to local community leaders and the media. This can yield support, understanding, and positive publicity for your plan and library.

Keeping Your Strategic Plan Current

If a public library is to remain as its community's lifelong learning center, it must remain dynamic in assessing its constituency's changing needs and in responding to them. That great library philosopher, S. R. Ranganathan, in his Fifth Law stated: "The library is a living organism."[2] A living thing grows, and we hope, improves as it matures. If the small public library is to grow and improve, it must continue to listen and respond to its community. It can do this via regular surveys, informal focus groups, consulting with community leaders, working the meetings, and building a representative board and staff. Use what you learn to update, vet, and disseminate your strategic plan as often as changes in the library service needs of your community dictate.

NOTES

1. Janny Scott, "Library Redevelopment Is Becoming One of Several Unorthodox Approaches to Producing Low-Priced Housing in Cities," *New York Times*, November 13, 2006.
2. S. R. Ranganathan, *The Five Laws of Library Science* (Madras, India: Madras Library Association; London: Edward Goldston, 1931).

CHAPTER FOUR

FUNDING YOUR LIBRARY'S PLAN

There may be some small public libraries that receive secure, substantial, and sustained funding from government or other sources so their administrators need not be concerned with raising money to ensure their library's survival. Alas, I am not one of this chosen group and I doubt if many readers are. In my home state of Pennsylvania and in many other areas, local government support of public libraries is inadequate and fund-raising, therefore, consumes a great deal of library trustee, staff, and volunteer effort. I personally spend about 50 percent of my time on finding money to support the library because only half of our support comes from government and we must generate the rest through in-house funding initiatives. This chapter will look at some of the techniques a small library can employ to remain in the money. Fund-raising resources are cited at the end of the chapter.

Of course, it should be noted that readers' situations will vary and that they should consult any appropriate legal and tax advisors when embarking on any fund-raising activities. In addition, it might be wise to check your library's bylaws or regulations before embarking on any fund-raising activities.

Obtaining Cash Resources

A public library needs a steady flow of cash funds to cover its day-to-day operations as well as to implement the objectives stated in its long-range strategic plan. It also needs cash reserves to cover major capital expenses as well as unforeseen exigencies. Therefore, if the library is to survive, its director, board, and volunteers must become proficient at fund-raising and devote a significant amount of time to this effort.

Money can come to a public library through a variety of channels, including government appropriations, direct donations, bequests, project grants, overdue fines, sales of goods, facility rental fees, recycling, fees for services, and event fees. With the exception of mandated government line-item funds earmarked for public libraries, the library will have to work at getting the money it needs. My advice is to be open-minded in considering potential fund-raising techniques. When people ask what fund-raising tools we have tried, I answer, only half in jest, "Everything except pay toilets and slot machines, so far."

Fund-raising in a small public library usually is shared among the library director (assisted by the senior staff members), the library trustees, and the Friends of the Library, a volunteer group established primarily to engage in fund-raising efforts. (See chapter 10 and appendix H for more on library Friends groups.) Some labor-intensive fund-raising efforts, such as book sales, auctions, antique appraisal fairs, and direct mail campaigns, require the formation of ad hoc teams of volunteer workers (often called "committees") to get the job done. In addition, some activities such as auctions or antique appraisal fairs may require skilled licensed auctioneers or appraisers who may donate their time.

Developing a Fund-Raising Plan

As with all important library activities, fund-raising should also have a structured strategic plan (see chapter 3) to ensure it is done in an efficient and effective manner. At a minimum, you should establish annual fund-raising objectives derived from your annual budget projections for needed income. It may prove desirable to develop a long-range fund-raising plan and incorporate it into your strategic plan, linking fund-raising objectives to the resource requirements and schedules for your various strategic objectives. As with any strategic plan, your fund-raising plan should have clearly delineated goals, objectives, strategies, and tactics, as well as assignments of leadership and work responsibilities. It should present defined schedules, resources needed, and expenditure budgets for fund-raising tasks. Be prepared to invest both time and money in your library's fund-raising efforts. If you need to hire paid consultants to advise and guide your fund-raising, then do it. The old saw that "you gotta spend some money to make some money" is most relevant here. Do not be afraid to consult with people who have fund-raising experience and to co-opt them to serve on your volunteer fund-raising committees. I have found that people with both not-for-profit fund-raising and industry marketing experience, particularly in direct sales, can give you much useful advice.

The total yield for your projected fund-raising activity plus any fixed government appropriations should add up to your projected total income. Break your fund-raising objectives down into tasks, giving each discrete fund-raising activity a dollar objective and timetable. Objectives should define expected gross income, costs of fund-raising, and net income. An example of how to state a fund-raising objective follows.

Objective: Raise $20,000 in cash from library patrons

Strategy: Direct mail solicitation

Tactics:

Generate 13,000 mailing labels from circulation system patron database using Giftworks software

Purchase bulk mail postal permit

Have board president write solicitation letter (within the parameters of any applicable bylaws or regulations governing your library)

Print 13,000 post-dated solicitation letters

Print 13,000 solicitation envelopes (with postal permit indicia) + return envelopes + donation cards

Stuff envelopes

Mail envelopes

Elapsed time:

One week for printing (January 23–30)

Two weeks for stuffing and mailing (February 1–15)

Two months for returns to come in (February 15–April 15)

Targeted mailing date: February 15

Expected response ratio: 10 percent

Expected average donation: $20

Estimated cost:

Postal permit: $150

Printing: $850

Postage: $2,000

Labor: Pro bono (volunteer)

Total estimated cost: $3,000

Expected gross return: $26,000

Expected net return: $23,000

Identifying Potential Donors and Soliciting Cash Donations

Donations can come from several sources, including government, businesses, foundations, associations, your patrons, and the community at large.

Government Funding Sources

Government tax dollars are a traditional mode of public library funding and are still the primary source of income for most public libraries. The NCES tells us that nationwide, 77.1 percent of library funding is local (i.e., municipal and county) and 12.8 percent is state funding.[1] Some fortunate libraries may automatically receive state, county, or municipal tax dollars as a result of legally mandated line-item appropriations earmarked for public libraries. These monies often have certain conditions or prerequisites attached to them, such as maintaining a minimum number of service hours per week, a minimum collection size, staff size, and certification or compliance with federal rules (e.g., Children's Internet Protection Act). In some states, submission of statistical and financial reports is also a prerequisite for receiving state funding. Certain categories of state funding may be in the form of reimbursements, incentives, or bonuses for providing certain types of extraordinary services, such as interlibrary loans or lending items to people who reside outside a library's service area. These monies can be yours for a minimal amount of effort, assuming that your library complies with the rules. For example, my library derives about $20,000 per year in state Access Pennsylvania program bonus money by allowing people residing outside of our defined service area to borrow our items.

In some parts of the country, financial support of public libraries by government is not mandated but is optional and has to be requested each year. This is true of Pennsylvania, where the municipal funding of local public libraries' operating expenses is discretionary. In this arena, the public library directly competes for local tax dollars with other public agencies such as the police, parks, and fire department. Furthermore, the subsidy amounts are seldom fixed, so in true zero-budgeting fashion, you essentially start anew from zero each year. In my library's case, each fall we have to request funding, one by one, from five separate municipalities. Some public libraries in my county have to solicit funds from as many as fifteen separate towns. In this type of environment a public library has to exercise creativity, diplomacy, marketing savvy, and perhaps even a little behind-the-scenes lobbying if it is to get its fair share of the pot.

Do not wait for your municipal governments to contact you to offer funding, because they may not. Instead, in late summer or early fall, check with the manager or secretary for each municipality you serve to determine the town's schedule and procedure for developing next year's budget, and ask that the library be put on the agenda when budget requests are being heard and reviewed. Be sure to ask how much time you will be allowed to speak (for example, we usually request twenty minutes to allow for questions and discussion). Work with your board of directors and, in particular, your treasurer to determine how much money you will need from each municipality next year in order for your library to satisfy your financial plan and budgetary needs. Collaboratively decide who will prepare and who will present the request for next year's funding to each municipal council. Prepare presentation packages to hand out to the municipal council decision makers. Because you can never be sure what audiovisual (AV) presentation facilities will be available at a rural town hall, I recommend an oral presentation, with paper information handouts as a backup. We employ a single-format factual request package for all five of our municipalities, but with a custom cover sheet for each town. Our municipal package typically consists of six pages:

- a cover sheet and outline
- an overview library status report that includes the year's highlights and accomplishments
- a summary library statistical use report broken down by patron municipality of residence

- a summary of the library's current-year actual financial figures
- a summary of the library's next-year expense budget projection
- a statement of funds requested from the municipality

Bring enough copies for both the town council and any audience members who may be present—you'll be gaining supporters among interested voters. It is a good idea to also provide a simple outline of your presentation (I like the bullet-chart format), so that the town council members and audience can easily follow your presentation and better grasp your message.

When making a library fund request presentation to a governmental body (be it local, county, state, or federal), there are a few basic guidelines that I have learned to go by. Above all, be specific as to what level of funding, or increase in funding, you desire. Do your homework before the meeting. Do some good old library research to get to know your officials, their backgrounds, and their hot buttons. If possible, try to make their acquaintance before the official meeting so you will not be a stranger when you officially stand before them. I have found it very useful to cultivate relationships with the town administrative managers and municipal council secretaries. This will not only help get your library a place on the municipal budget hearing agenda, but can also enable you to get off-the-record advice on how much money might be available to you and how you might best go about asking for it. If you can get these folks to view your library as a public service and you as a public servant, they will be glad to advise you and, perhaps, pave the way with the town supervisors.

The content of your presentation should be well thought out in advance and reviewed by your library board and senior staff. In preparing and presenting a request for funding, do not be shy. Beating around the bush and being coy does not really work with politicians who are working against a tight agenda (and budget), are hearing many competing requests for funds, and do not really have the time or inclination to dwell upon and analyze subtle or vague requests. Politely suggest just how much you would like the municipality to give you and why. Explaining a cause and effect is useful (i.e., if you give us the requested money we will be able to do this for your constituents, and if you do not give us the money, your voters will be denied that).

Of course, always be mindful of any activity that, however well-intentioned, might be misinterpreted as being unethical. It's always wise to avoid doing anything that looks even a little bit like a conflict of interest.

There are several ways to specify how much money you need from a government body:

- as a total dollar amount
- as a percentage increase over last year's appropriation
- as a per capita total amount based on population

I like to use the per capita request because it helps you keep pace with population growth and reminds them that the money will be spent on citizen benefits. If your state library has a minimum municipal or county per capita library support recommendation, use it as a basis for requesting support. Pennsylvania, for example, cites $5.00 per capita as a minimum municipal support recommendation. Cite national averages and how you compare. The NCES publication *Public Libraries in the United States: Fiscal Year 2004* cites the U.S. national average per capita operating expenditure for public libraries as $30.49.[2] By state, the highest average per capita operating expenditure was in Ohio at $53.12 and the lowest was in Mississippi at $13.24. For municipalities, Port Washington (New York) takes the prize with well over $100 per capita in library support. If it helps your case, cite these figures in your funding requests. Don't be afraid to aim high. You may get less than you request, but you will usually get something if you make a request at a public meeting with voters who support you in the audience.

In your funding request, use statistics to prove that your library is being well used by the politicians' constituents. Cite data such as the number of library cardholders as a percentage of total population (i.e., your market penetration), library visits, reference queries, and circulation. These data can be very convincing, especially if they demonstrate a growth trend. Another useful statistic in dealing with politicians is return on investment (ROI) for the library. Try to demonstrate how each dollar they give you yields more than a dollar in increased or matching county, state, or other financial aid and in valuable services to community residents and businesses. By using this approach, I am able to show our municipal supervisors that each dollar they give us generates an additional $3.17 in matching county and state aid for the benefit of their constituents. This is an impressive ROI in anyone's book!

When going before a governmental body to request funds, try not to go alone. If possible, have members of your board, staff, library Friends, and volunteers who reside (and vote) in the community in question join you and be sure to introduce them, even if they do not speak. Invite supportive library patrons who live in the community to attend as members of the audience and to speak out as advocates if appropriate. A chorus of voters in the background singing your library's praises will impress the elected officials. At one municipal budget hearing in a town that had never provided any library support, the township board of supervisors was very negative toward my request for library funding. However, when several voters present in the audience rose up during the public comment period and strongly demanded that the public library receive support, the borough supervisors relented and voted a modest stipend for the library. This has been sustained and increased over the subsequent years.

Keep in mind that newspaper reporters often cover budget hearings. Consequently, you may want to cite some human-interest stories in your presentation to both impress the politicians and attract favorable press attention to your need. I learned this by accident. At a municipal budget presentation, I cited how my public library fills gaps in community education. As an example, I mentioned that we had begun to teach introductory Spanish courses for youth and teens in answer to appeals from parents who were concerned that the local school district had abandoned foreign language instruction in middle school as an economy measure. The next day, a reporter who had heard my presentation the night before called me and conducted a twenty-minute phone interview. This resulted in a feature article about our library's support of community learning in the leading daily newspaper. Though obtained through serendipity, this kind of favorable press coverage is priceless to a library seeking funds and community support.

Do not overlook state legislators themselves as sources of government funding for public libraries. In some states, for example, legislators receive a certain amount of tax dollars for discretionary projects in their districts. In Pennsylvania this is popularly known as WAM, short for "walking around money." Contact your local state legislators and ask if they have any discretionary funds available. My library obtained $5,000 in WAM in this way.

Nongovernmental Donors

A good source of donations for your library is your community at large. The three basic market segments to approach here are your current patrons, the business community, and foundations and philanthropists. All are equally important. Solicitation strategies are discussed below, but first let's look at the donor groups.

SOLICITING DONATIONS FROM LIBRARY PATRONS

Directing your fund-raising efforts toward those who use your library is important for two reasons. The first is obvious—it can bring in needed money. The second is a bit subtler. By asking patrons to help support your activities, you are reminding them that it costs money to run a public library and that what government gives you just ain't enough to pay all the bills. In addition, when someone makes a contribution, no matter how modest, it creates in them a sense of partnership and belonging with the library.

There are three primary modes of soliciting funds from patrons:

- donation jars strategically placed in your library
- event fees
- direct solicitation campaigns (see "Solicitation Campaign Strategies and Tactics" below)

Library donation jars may be of two types, permanent and ad hoc. My library maintains permanent donation receptacles at the circulation desk, in the children's area (for kids' coins), and in our two event rooms. We empty these at least once a week but always leave some "seed money" to encourage further donations. On occasion, we will set up a collection jar for a special purpose. For example, a local tourist railroad donated a fairly expensive Thomas the Tank Engine play table to our children's area. This item became very popular with toddlers and juveniles and was so heavily used that it virtually fell apart after a couple of years, and we were forced to remove it. It was immediately missed, and we received so many "Where's Thomas?" questions that I had to put up a sign saying, "Thomas is out sick but he will be back as soon as we can find the money to make him better." To my surprise, a parent came to me and offered a five-dollar bill toward Thomas's recovery. With this encouragement, I got an old pretzel jar, cut a slit in the cap, and hung on it a sign stating, "Thomas had to be removed because he was broken, but your donations can help repair him and bring him back." The jar received over $400 in donations in two weeks. This allowed us to refurbish and reinstall the Thomas table at a little ceremony attended by kids, parents, and grandparents (who were the biggest donors).

A nagging question among public librarians is whether it is appropriate to charge patrons for program attendance. There are three basic schools of thought here:

1. We are a "free public library" and should charge no fees.
2. It's OK to charge a fee to recover out-of-pocket costs.
3. Use events as fund-raisers and charge what the traffic will bear to support other "free" library activities.

All of these views are valid, and which one you adopt depends on your library's particular situation and on the purpose of the specific event. At my library, we let the event's purpose determine if we charge and what to charge.

In general, a cost imposed on an activity may act as a barrier to attendance and may deter some people from participating. There is a marketing principle known as "price elasticity of demand" which simply states that people will pay whatever is asked if they want something badly enough. While this might apply to the wealthy who must have their Mercedes and their Armani clothes, it seldom fits typical library patrons. Therefore, we impose no fee if we believe a program is really needed by a community market segment (e.g., an ESL course for immigrants) and we want as many as possible to attend and benefit. On the other hand, we do impose a nominal "materials fee" on certain events such as cooking and art classes to recover library expenses. Occasionally one might plan an event specifically as a fund-raiser, such as a benefit banquet. Here it would be acceptable to charge attendees a premium amount as long as they realize that a donation is built in.

There is a middle ground between free and fee events. You can strategically place donation boxes around your community events room and suggest at the beginning and end of each event that freewill donations are welcomed to defray costs, though the donations are not mandatory.

BUSINESS DONOR SOLICITING

Your service area's businesses represent a tremendous potential for public library support that can be tapped by the application of some strategic marketing tactics. Start by developing a "prospect" list of all businesses and not-for-profit institutions in your region. As input sources you can use chamber of commerce directories, the Yellow

Pages, business expo programs, and business cards you collect by walking through your main street's shopping area. We also find the place mats at diners that contain "tombstone" box ads for local businesses to be another good source of names.

Business soliciting is best done face-to-face and, to a lesser extent, by telephone. Use a personal letter only if you cannot reach the principal contact by other means.

Businesses generally will donate to a public library to gain community recognition and goodwill, which, they hope, will ultimately lead to increased patronage. Therefore, in almost all cases business donors desire public recognition of their gifts. You can do this via a "donor appreciation" display in your lobby and by newspaper box advertisements recognizing significant donations (usually $1,000 or more). A nice touch is to provide a "library donor appreciation" certificate, which can be framed and displayed. You can generate these certificates using standard computer publishing packages such as PrintMaster.

Keep in mind that many businesses, particularly the larger ones, like to make their donations at certain times of the year. Learn their schedules and time your soliciting to coincide with them. We schedule our business direct mail solicitation for the fourth calendar quarter to facilitate end-of-year tax deductions.

FOUNDATION SOLICITING

In considering prospective foundation donors, look first to local and then to national organizations. You may find that there are a variety of local family, business, and community foundations that are seeking educational institutions, such as a public library, worthy of their support. You should be able to identify these foundations through local newspapers and directories, and by referrals from your community's bankers, lawyers, clergymen, and investment advisors. Typically, local foundations donate lesser amounts but have simpler application procedures than the larger national foundations. Furthermore, there is usually less competition for local foundation awards than for those at the national level. Local philanthropies often prefer a more personal touch and may visit the requester's site. (For more information about foundation soliciting, see chapter 7 on grant writing.)

On occasion, local foundations have been known to make large donations to major capital projects. For example, in the case of my own library, the SICO Foundation, established by a local fuel oil company, donated more than $400,000 to our building fund.

There are a number of well-known national foundations that have made major contributions to public libraries, such as the Bill and Melinda Gates Foundation, the Lila Wallace Foundation, and the Dollar General Foundation. Check specific foundation and grant websites (e.g., the *Chronicle of Philanthropy*'s Guide to Grants, at http://www .philanthropy.com/grants/) to identify opportunities and see if their criteria are relevant to your needs and situation. Chapter 7, the bibliography, and appendix A provide guidelines on foundation grant-seeking and list information sources on foundations and grants.

INSTITUTIONAL AND ASSOCIATION SOLICITING

In almost every community in the United States, there is a variety of service orga-nizations, fraternal orders, clubs, associations, unions, and religious and other not-for-profit groups that represent potential donors to your public library. A library should not eschew soliciting donations from the local not-for-profit community. We regu-larly receive donations of cash as well as gifts in kind from churches, associations, and service clubs. The new public library in one of our neighboring towns was built using a $1 million donation from a nearby Masonic nursing home.

I have discovered that many of these organizations have set aside funds for doing good works and are on the lookout for worthy organizations and activities to support. The secret is to find them and let them know that you need their assistance. Let me give you some examples of what has worked for my public library, and some pointers on approaching these types of benefactors:

- service clubs
- churches
- youth groups
- labor unions
- professional associations
- national award competitions

Service clubs. Most service clubs are created for the expressed purpose of collect-ing money and fielding volunteers to support community activities. As a bona fide community institution, the public library certainly qualifies for their support. Contact such organizations as the Rotary Club, Lions, Kiwanis, Veterans of Foreign Wars, American Legion, Masons, chamber of commerce, Moms Club, and so on, and let them know what your needs are, both financial and volunteer labor. We have found that these groups will readily come forward to assist the library with cash gifts and volunteers to staff library events. For example, my personal involvement with our local Lions Club has given me the opportunity to apprise its members of our state's public library funding crisis. The word has spread, and as a result the Lions district governor has offered to provide every public library in a two-county region with funds to pur-chase magnifying readers for the vision-impaired, an area of Lions concern.

Churches. Churches and libraries share many common goals in support of learning and ethical values. Let your community's churches and church schools know of your needs and activities and they will provide support and publicity for your programs. For example, when state aid to public libraries was cut in 2003, our local Catholic church sent a $500 cash donation, stating we needed it more than they did. An evangelical Christian church in our area regularly marshals a supervised youth group to come to the library and perform needed chores.

Youth groups. Supervised youth groups can provide valuable library support, particularly as a source of enthusiastic volunteer labor. Scouts, church youth, and service club youth are always looking for community service projects, and the library represents an ideal venue for this. We have had both Boy and Girl Scout groups perform chores (such as outdoor maintenance), and several Eagle Scout candidates have earned merit badges working at the library. One high school Key Club donated the proceeds of their book sale to the library, and another provides volunteers to act as support staff at key events. A fringe benefit of these volunteer efforts is that they bring teens into the library.

Labor unions and professional associations. Do not overlook unions as potential supporters of your library. Contact those whose areas of interest are close to yours, such as those in public service like educators, police, and health. Unions may have funds for charitable support or may be seeking causes to support. For example, when they learned of my library's need for money, the teachers' union in our school district voluntarily instituted a payroll deduction program to collect funds to be donated to the public library. Each year library officials are invited to the union's retirement breakfast, where we are ceremoniously presented with a check for several thousand dollars by the union president. This has prompted other union members to make personal donations to the library in memory of departed colleagues or to honor retirees. In another case, our county's speaker's bureau has donated several thousand dollars to purchase books on public speaking for public libraries.

National award competitions. I am including national award competitions here because they are a way to get both funding for projects and recognition for your library. The American Library Association and its many divisions bestow approximately sixty awards annually. These are listed on the ALA's website (www.ala.org) under the "Awards and Scholarships" tab, as well as in *Library Journal, School Library Journal,* and *American Libraries.* There are also many organizations that hold ad hoc and regular cash award competitions open to public libraries. In addition, if your library director is enrolled in any of the public library national or state electronic discussion lists or blogs, the director should receive frequent notices of pending award competitions. These awards can be fun and useful. For example, I was interested in improving the science collections and programs in my library, so I paid attention to a notice of a national competition sponsored by WGBH public television in Boston to select twelve public libraries to be "Einstein Outreach Centers" to celebrate the centennial anniversary of the theory of relativity. We submitted a four-page e-proposal and were selected as one of the dozen winners. As a result, we received a grant to buy science materials for our collections and lesson plans for six fun science programs for both children and adults. We built these programs in collaboration with local science educators and scientists and received good press coverage. The award grant also covered travel expenses to attend an orientation seminar at an ALA Annual Conference.

Solicitation Campaign Strategies and Tactics

Once you have identified your fund-raising targets, you can consider strategies and tactics to use to approach these potential donors and win them over. There are three general methods used in the direct solicitation of funds: (1) face-to-face, (2) telephone, and (3) direct mail. In addition to these "generic" solicitation methods, funds may be requested for a specific purpose such as a memorial or bequest or to sponsor an event. A practical rule for small libraries is to employ face-to-face and telephone soliciting for the largest potential donors such as noted philanthropists, foundations, or major corporations, and direct mail for mass solicitations, such as those directed at your patrons. All five techniques are discussed below.

Face-to-Face Soliciting

A request for funds made in person is the most effective fund-raising technique, especially if the parties are acquainted with each other. Success ratios of 50 percent can be achieved here. It is, however, the most labor-intensive, time-consuming, and difficult of solicitation techniques. It requires skilled and gently persuasive solicitors who either call in advance to set appointments or who make cold calls to the homes of individuals or to business establishments. Alternatively, you can approach patrons as they visit your library, but this can be a hit-or-miss process. To be effective, face-to-face soliciting requires that solicitors be trained in advance by memorizing carefully prepared solicitation scripts and honing their "pitch" in dry-run rehearsals. Finding trainers and solicitors with prior direct sales experience will give you a head start in this activity.

To be most effective, you should employ highly placed library volunteers such as trustees or library Friends officers to do your face-to-face soliciting, because they will have the greatest "convincing credibility." Although senior library staff may be quite capable of performing this solicitation task, in general, requests from volunteers are more effective than those from "hired hands" who may be perceived as having vested interests. Prior acquaintance with the potential donor is also very important. If someone on your library's staff, board, or volunteer group is personally acquainted with the "prospect," bring him or her along on the visit.

If a donation or pledge is not received at the time of visit, be sure to send a follow-up letter immediately after the visit, and then make a follow-up phone call within two weeks to ask if any decision has been made. Obviously, libraries may find it very difficult to find a team of volunteers who feel comfortable doing direct solicitation and who will be willing to invest the significant time and effort involved in training and field visitations. Consequently, few small public libraries will employ direct solicitation as a mass fund-raising tool. It is therefore a technique to be used selectively for soliciting large donations.

Telephone Soliciting

Telephone soliciting is similar to direct, face to face fund raising except the request for funds is made over the telephone instead of in person. Telephone fund-raising is not as effective as face-to-face, and a success ratio of 25 percent is seldom exceeded here. In training phone solicitors, scripts similar to those used in face-to-face soliciting are employed. Telephone solicitor recruiting and training require about the same levels of effort as personal soliciting, but many more telephone requests can be made per day than personal visits. A follow-up letter or phone call is advisable. Again, it may be hard to find volunteers who feel capable and willing to be phone solicitors.

Direct Mail Soliciting

Though less effective than either personal or telephone soliciting, the direct mail campaign is the most commonly used mass fund-raising technique in small public libraries because it is the least labor-intensive. Success ratios with direct mail are typically under 10 percent. Nevertheless, because of its economy, this technique is the backbone of much public library fund-raising, so it is worthy of some discussion here. My library generates between 10 and 20 percent of its annual income through direct mail. Here are some direct mail pointers.

An effective direct mail solicitation package normally contains four basic pieces:

1. A mailing envelope addressed to the donor
2. The solicitation letter
3. A donor reply card
4. A return envelope addressed to the library

Some libraries use a tear-off tab on the return envelope instead of a separate reply card to reduce bulk.

Use your patron files and business prospect lists to generate a mailing list for your campaign. You can usually obtain a business listing from the local chamber of commerce or even create one from directories in the library such as the Yellow Pages. Include the name of the business owner in the address if you can find it.

Hand-addressing solicitation envelopes is always a nice personal touch, but if the sheer volume precludes this, it is acceptable to use computer-generated labels or envelope printing. We use computer-generated labels produced via Microsoft Excel software because we send out about 10,000 envelopes in our annual mail campaign and do not have either the staff or volunteers to do hand-addressing.

I prefer to use standard white number 10 business envelopes for my mailings, preimprinted with the library's return address. This size can hold a folded letter, a reply card, and a number 6 return envelope and still keep the total weight under one ounce to save on postage. Selection of postage rate is a topic debated among not-for-profit fund-raisers. Employing a not-for-profit bulk rate permit (you can apply for one and pay an annual fee of about $150 at your local post office) is the least expensive mode, costing about a third to a half of normal first-class mail rates. However, to obtain the bulk mail rate, you have to meet certain conditions. Each outgoing envelope must be preprinted with a postage "indicia" box giving your permit number and issuing post office location. The volume of your mailing will need to meet certain minimum thresholds, usually 200 pieces or more. You will have to sort your addressed outgoing envelopes by ZIP code, label them, and place them in special post office–provided mailing trays, which you must then deliver to a post office to be weighed and counted to determine the total cost. The U.S. Postal Service will not accept credit card payment for bulk mailings, so you must pay only by check or cash. This means bringing a blank check or a pocket full of cash with you when you deliver your trays to the post office.

Furthermore, there are some who say that potential donors who receive bulk mail envelopes may discard them as junk mail without opening them. This is why some direct mail solicitations employ a bulk mail stick-on postage stamp (instead of a printed indicia box) to fool the recipient into thinking it is a first-class letter. My library has evolved a compromise here. We employ first-class postage and a more personal approach for our 500-letter business and institutional mail campaign, and use bulk rate mailing for our 8,000–9,000-letter patron direct mail solicitation. You will have to decide what is best for your library based on your mailing budget, mailing volume, and your perception of the community as tempered by experience.

Carefully craft your solicitation letter to clearly present your message and appeal within a single page. (See appendix C for a sample solicitation letter and donor reply card.) It is advisable to have the letter signed by the highest-ranking member of the library hierarchy, such as the president of the board or equivalent. Personally addressed and signed letters are great, and if your president is willing and you can afford the software or labor to do this, then by all means do so. However, if you are sending out thousands of letters on a shoestring budget, you may have to compromise and use a "Dear Library Patron" or "Dear Business Leader" generic salutation and a printed signature. We create a special letterhead each year for our annual mail campaigns. It lists all members of our board and staff on the page bottom and cites all the municipalities we serve on the top. We do this to remind donors that the library is operated by real people serving real communities (i.e., their neighbors and friends). Use a nice-quality paper, but not too nice. I have found that some donors will react negatively if they perceive you are wasting "their" donation money on luxuries such as expensive watermarked rag bond paper. A "lean and mean" frugal image usually works better with donors.

In your solicitation letter's body, identify any special financial situations or needs that make this year's donation important. We have cited such factors as cutbacks in government aid, growth or changing patterns in library usage, the need to replace worn-out or obsolete equipment, and unsatisfied community learning needs. If you have good reason to, it is acceptable (and desirable) to brag in your fund-raising solicitation letter. Cite awards or honors your library has won. Donors like to know you are doing your job well and that their money will not be wasted. People tend to donate more to "winners" who they know will employ their donations effectively and efficiently.

For example, shortly after the Bill and Melinda Gates Foundation and *Library Journal* named my library the Best Small Library in America, two local foundations came to us unsolicited and made cash donations to help us "keep up the good work." We now cite our awards in our fund-raising solicitations to encourage more donations in this vein.

Your donor reply card should be simple and contain check blocks with suggested donation levels (e.g., $25–$5,000), including a nondefined block to be filled in by those who cannot afford $25 or those who want to donate more than $5,000. Include blocks for the donor's name, address, and phone number. Optionally, you may want to include check blocks asking if the person would like to donate securities, become a library volunteer (or Friend), or if the person would like his gift to be anonymous. We ask the latter question because it is our custom to publish the names of our donors (but not the amounts they donate), and some benefactors prefer to remain unpublicized. Your reply card can be separate, printed on card stock, or can be printed as a tear-off portion of the return envelope, whichever you or your printer prefer.

The donor reply envelope should be preprinted with the library's address. However, whether or not you should include return postage is debatable. We have done it both ways and have found that some donors seemed to appreciate it, while others chided us for wasting money on postage that they would gladly cover.

Getting a mass mailing out is an exercise in careful planning, logistics, and staffing. Once you have set the date for your mailing (see below), you will need to work backward in time to ensure all your ducks are in order. Based on your mailing list count, you will have to arrange for the printing of sufficient quantities of preprinted envelopes, solicitation letters, and reply cards. Rather than burn up the library's copiers, we contract out our volume printing to a local print shop that gives us a special not-for-profit rate.

If you send your letters out as bulk mail, you will need to get the bulk postal permit sufficiently in advance so you can preprint the permit number (indicia) on your mailing envelopes. You will also have to request a supply of bulk mailing trays from your post office, along with tray labels and instructions on how to sort the letters by ZIP code (e.g., by 3 digits, 5 digits, or 9 digits) to get the bulk postal rate you desire. The general rule is that the more digits you presort by, the lower the postage rate.

You will also need to instruct your computer gurus on how and when you want your mailing lists printed out and provide them with the mailing list database in the proper format (e.g., Microsoft Excel), an appropriate supply of mailing labels or envelopes, and a computer printer with a fresh print cartridge. You really have to start planning a direct mail campaign several months in advance because it can easily take two to three months of elapsed time to get all of these preliminary tasks accomplished.

Once you have all of your mailing materials in hand, you will then need to round up an envelope-stuffing crew and set up a large-enough area to house what I call "an envelope-stuffing bee" assembly line. For our annual patron mailings of up to 10,000 pieces, we employ a team of about ten community volunteers who accomplish the envelope stuffing within a week. These volunteers are a mixed bunch that includes members of the library's board, Friends group, and the community at large. Some come as a team, such as the eight teenage members of the local high school's Kiwanis Key Club who showed up after school one afternoon and stuffed 4,000 letters in two hours!

We allow our volunteers to do our envelope stuffing either in the library or as homework. In the library, we dedicate one of our conference rooms to this task. According to a schedule set by our library's volunteer coordinator, we set up an assembly line on long tables where people at various stations affix mailing labels, fold letters, and stuff, seal, and tray sort envelopes in sequence. We also let some people take batches of materials home where they can perform all these operations at their leisure and then return completed sealed envelopes to the library, where they are placed in the appropriate trays. The filled trays of envelopes, sorted by ZIP code, are then transported to the post office along with the completed bulk rate forms and a blank signed check from our treasurer to cover the total postage cost, which is calculated at time of mailing at the post office.

The U.S. Postal Service treats bulk mail as a low priority, and your mailing may sit at a postal facility for an indeterminate period before it is delivered. Therefore, if you want to know when your letters are actually delivered, "seed" the mailing with a letter or two to yourself.

Finally, experience has shown us that the scheduling of mailings can be important and can have significant effects on the amount of money donated to your library. Because of timing issues, we have found it effective to do two separate direct mail solicitations, one to businesses and another to library patrons. Businesses seem to prefer to make their charitable donations in the fourth quarter of the calendar year, when their annual profit projection is fairly firm and they can take an end-of-year tax deduction. Our annual business mailings therefore usually go out in October or November. On the other hand, individuals seem to prefer to make their donations in the late first quarter of the calendar year, after the holiday expenses are paid off and before the summer vacation expenses begin. We therefore schedule our patron direct mail campaign for February or March. You may want to determine what is best for your situation by both consulting with your community and through experimentation, by comparing the rates of return versus date for various solicitation mailings.

Memorials, Bequests, and Naming

A very important source of public library funding is the memorial bequest or gift. I believe this to be a uniquely North American custom, as I have not observed this type of giving elsewhere in the world. This sponsorship can range from funding the purchase of a book in memory of a departed loved one to funding the construction of an entire library building. Putting a donor's name on a building, room, program, chair, or book is a powerful funding magnet. Indeed, my own institution, the Milanof-Schock Library in Mount Joy, Pennsylvania, was constructed in 1999 with bequests from the estates of two late local residents, Ann Milanof and Clarence Schock. Our small rural community could scarcely have afforded to construct such a beautiful new $1.2 million library without these memorial naming gifts.

Another custom that has gained acceptance in our community is to have the departed person's family include a statement in the newspaper obituary requesting that memorial donations be made to the public library in lieu of flowers. This practice was started by families of deceased educators and library volunteers and has yielded collective memorial donations of thousands of dollars. The surviving families really appreciate receiving lists of memorial donations in honor of their departed loved ones and in having a section of the library or of its collection dedicated to the departed individual. When we do such a dedication, we invite the family to a memorial ceremony at the library, sometimes held in connection with an event such as the annual library volunteer appreciation dinner.

One should also accept donations to honor the living. In the tradition of the Festschrift, our library gladly accepts donations to purchase books in honor of a major personal milestone event such as a birthday, anniversary, graduation, or wedding. To preserve collection integrity, we allow donors to specify the honor book's subject, genre, or author but normally not a specific title. We advise donors of our selected title and include in it an appropriate honorific bookplate. This has become quite popular with donors honoring family birthdays from eight to eighty.

A public library can advise the public that memorial donations or honorifics are acceptable via a discreetly worded brochure in its display rack, such as the sample shown in appendix E.

Event or Publication Sponsorships

Some organizations and individuals prefer to donate monies to sponsor a specific event or library publication rather than provide a discretionary gift. You can capitalize on this by allowing for earmarked donations within certain boundaries. For example, the Kiwanis Club in our area prefers that its donations of both money and volunteers be used in support of children's events at the library, and this works fine for us. In another context, at our annual benefit auction, we allow organizations that don't have an item to donate to the sale to sponsor the auction tent, program printing, or space advertising. We also allow an investment club that uses our meeting room to sponsor several of our financial periodical subscriptions. If your library issues publications such as periodic newsletters, you can also offer sponsorship of issues to cover printing costs. All sponsorships should be appropriately (and publicly) acknowledged.

Earning Money through Fee-Based Services

Free public library purists may reject the concept of charging the public for services provided, with the possible exception of collecting overdue book fines. In my mind, however, the need to ensure the survival of our public libraries in a time of inadequate tax support dictates that we consider and use this funding approach. In fact, outside of the United States, most "public libraries" do indeed impose use fees on their patrons.

Since most public libraries are not-for-profit organizations, they must be certain that any fee-based activities they engage in do not jeopardize their tax-exempt status. If you are unsure, check the IRS 501(c)(3) regulations and consult with a tax specialist. The activities I cite below have been employed either by my own public library or observed at other public libraries with no adverse tax effects, to my knowledge. These include the following:

1. Copying, printing, faxing
2. Meeting room rental
3. Selling surplus books and more at a bookstore and on the Internet
4. Selling computer discs
5. Recycling services
6. Proctoring of exams
7. Passport application processing
8. Passport photos service
9. Selling "twofer" coupon books
10. Contract research, consulting, and data compilation
11. Book and calendar publishing
12. Selling food and drink

Each of these activities is discussed in detail below.

Copying, Printing, and Faxing

Public library patrons appreciate and even demand public copying machines and computer printers. My library provides and charges for copies made on a coin-operated copier and public online computer printer. We offer these primarily as services to patrons rather than as moneymakers. However, with the economies we have achieved by buying bulk copy paper at wholesale prices and buying remanufactured printer cartridges on eBay, we do make a modest surplus on each copy sold. We sell over 30,000 copies per year, so even a few cents per copy can add up. To free library staff from the burden of collecting fees for patron computer printouts, we recently installed an automated payment system known as VendaPrint which seems to work well.

Some libraries also offer coin-operated fax machines as a service to patrons. This however, may not suit smaller libraries because the vendors who lease these machines may require guarantees of 10,000 or more pages per year.

Renting Meeting Rooms

If your library has one or more conference rooms, you may want to consider renting them to local community groups when they are not needed for library events. However, to avoid future problems, it is important to first develop a formal board-approved policy and fee schedule governing the rental and use of your library's meeting rooms.

The policy should clearly state that library events have priority for meeting room usage. Also, check your library's liability insurance policy to ensure that meeting room rental is covered. Consider limiting meeting room use to local groups that you know in order to avoid bad publicity and disturbances, such as that experienced by the York (Pennsylvania) public library in 2002 when it naively allowed a neo-Nazi hate group to hold a membership rally in its meeting room.

Consider also having room renters provide insurance guarantees or liability waivers and accept responsibility for damages. These precautions are important not only to protect your library's tax-exempt status and reputation, but also to avoid security and liability challenges and expense. Sample policies can be obtained by searching the Internet for "library policies" via a search engine such as Google or MetaCrawler. You should also check out the library policies on the website of the Washington Municipal Research and Services Center (http://www.mrsc.org/subjects/infoserv/publiclib/libpolicy.aspx?r=1), the ALA website under the "Policies" link, and published manuals such as those noted in the bibliography.

My library has three meeting rooms, which we rent for modest fees ranging from $25 to $75 per two-hour session. We have two separate price schedules, one for not-for-profit and one for for-profit renters. We charge a bit extra for use of our kitchen, computer equipment, projectors, or video player, as well as for room cleanup if necessary. We do offer a fee waiver to not-for-profit groups that cannot pay the room rental fee, and this wins much goodwill and support in lieu of cash. We sometimes barter for the use of our conference rooms. When a local computer instructor inquired about renting our computer lab to teach classes to her clients, we offered to let her use the room gratis in return for her teaching free computer courses to library patrons. This symbiotic relationship is now in its second year.

Selling at a Bookstore and on the Internet

The sale of surplus library materials in the library or at book sales is an established public library fund-raising practice. I will cover regular in-library sales here and the larger annual book sales in the next chapter.

Virtually every library accrues a stock of surplus used books, periodicals, and AV materials resulting from either collection weeding or donations from the community. Selling these via a display in the library or, if you have the room, a library bookshop, is a good way to generate extra income and provide an additional benefit for library visitors. This is an excellent fund-raising activity for volunteer Friends of the Library groups to undertake. At the request of our library's Friends group, we made a small room off our lobby available for them to use as a bookstore. The enterprising Friends expanded their inventory beyond used books by adding the products of local artists and crafters on consignment, which they sell at a 30 percent commission. They have also created library mementos such as book bags, key chains, bracelets, wooden replicas of the library, and T-shirts, which they sell at modest markups. This bookstore is staffed by volunteers and generates a steady income stream for the library from a loyal customer base among library patrons. People find it to be a great place for unique gifts, and homeschool parents use it as a source of textbooks.

A valuable adjunct to selling books in the library bookstore is selling books on the Internet through one or more of the online auction or bookseller services such as eBay, Amazon.com, Alibris, and so on. Our procedure for this involves a knowledgeable volunteer who screens withdrawn and donated books and selects those of a "collectible" nature. These include author-signed copies, first editions, and antique editions. Using a surplus computer installed in our bookstore, the volunteer prepares and uploads the descriptions and digital photos of the items to be sold via an online vendor. A minimum price for each item is set after consulting current prices for the title on such online book sales and pricing sites as BookFinder (www.bookfinder.com) and AddALL (www.addall.com). Although our Friends at first doubted the value of selling books online, they began to think differently after they sold a few titles on eBay for more than $100 each, versus the average of $5 per title derived from library bookstore sales. Some pointers on selling collector books can be found in appendix D, as well as in the online bookselling manuals listed in the bibliography.

Selling Computer Discs

You can derive a modest amount of income and provide a service to patrons by selling computer floppy discs and recordable CD-ROMs to library computer users, to allow them to save their data. Our library charges fifty cents for a floppy disc and one dollar for a CDW CD-ROM, which we purchase wholesale from office suppliers.

Recycling

You can help the environment and generate funds for your library by recycling such things as computer printer cartridges and cell phones. There are recycling firms that specialize in working with not-for-profits such as public libraries, schools, and churches. You can find these via a search on the Internet or by asking other not-for-profits whom they work with. Typically, the recycling firm will provide you with everything you need to get started, including public donation collection boxes, signs, and postage-paid return shipping boxes. Inform your local businesses and institutions about your recycling program so they can donate their recyclables to your library. Each month, two national firms based in our area donate vanloads of recyclable cartridges to our library. We earn up to $10 per printer cartridge and $10 per cell phone that we recycle through an outfit known as the Funding Factory, which generates more than $1,000 per year for us. This is also a good activity to delegate to a Friends group volunteer.

Proctoring of Exams

There are students who take correspondence or online courses that require them to take remote proctored examinations. Educational institutions that engage in this practice range from trade schools to university graduate schools. In most instances, the institutions list public library staff as acceptable proctors, so these students will seek you out. The proctor usually receives a sealed exam packet with instructions from the school. You give the exam kit to the student in the library at a mutually agreed-upon time, monitor the test-taker, time the exam, collect the completed exam, and mail it back to the school. We do not charge a formal fee for proctoring but rather suggest a "donation" of $50, which most students consider a bargain since universities typically charge $80 per hour for proctoring.

Passport Application Processing

A relatively new high-yield fund-raising activity for American public libraries is serving as a U.S. passport application acceptance agency for the U.S. State Department. The State Department started recruiting public libraries as its agents in 2002 because the post offices and county clerks who had traditionally provided these services were unable to satisfy the public's demand for evening and weekend service. A passport acceptance agency accepts a person's passport application on behalf of the government, verifies the applicant's identity and citizenship, collects the application fees, and forwards the application package and fees to the nearest U.S. State Department Passport Agency office. The procedure takes about fifteen minutes per application. The library is authorized to charge a fixed fee per application for this service that was twenty-five dollars at the time of this writing. To qualify as a passport acceptance agent, a library needs to be able to send one or more staff members to a half-day course taught by the U.S. government or have them take an online course. The government provides all forms, and the library's only expenses are labor, mailing envelopes, and first-class postage.

As mentioned previously, in 2002 we became the first public library passport acceptance agency in our region. We have derived two benefits by providing this service: (1) it brings potential patrons to the library; and (2) it earns a relatively large amount of money for a nominal amount of work.

For example, of the thousands of people who have come to our library to apply for passports over the past five years, about 50 percent did not hold library cards, and we manage to sign up many of these. On the financial side, we earn approximately $50,000 per year in passport application fees. We have expanded our service to also offer passport photos in the library using an instant camera (at $10 a sitting), and this earns another $5,000 per year. Our Friends group bought us a special passport camera for about $500 in response to public demand.

Because of this windfall passport income, my library was one of the few in Pennsylvania that did not have to curtail service and lay off staff when the state cut public library support in 2003. Our success as a passport agency prompted four other public libraries in our county to also start processing these documents. One of these libraries now earns over $100,000 per year in passport fees. Earnings can be even greater; it was reported that the Ferguson Library in Stamford, Connecticut, grosses over $250,000 per year in passport application fees! The Ferguson also opened a coffee shop (see "Selling Food and Drink" below) to accommodate passport applicants, and this yields an additional $100,000 per year in sales.

A public library interested in becoming a passport acceptance agency should contact its nearest U.S. State Department Passport Agency via the "Blue Pages" government section of the telephone directory.

Selling "Twofer" Coupon Books

Another fund-raising technique that is popular among not-for-profits (including libraries) is the selling of "entertainment" coupon books which provide certificates offering two meals or two admissions for the price of one at local restaurants, theaters, amusements, and hotels. The books are offered for a specific city or county region. The system is simple. You buy a quantity of the books (usually 100 or more) at about $10 and resell them for $20. The downside is that the coupons usually expire in nine months to a year, and if not promptly sold their value will diminish till they are worthless.

Contract Research

Most states require their public libraries to provide basic ready-reference services at no charge as a condition of receiving state aid. However, if your state and local library codes permit it and your library's board does not object, you may be able to offer extended research, reporting, consulting, and data compilation services to local businesses and researchers for a fee. We generally consider a research request that can be answered within fifteen minutes as a "ready reference" and anything beyond that as an extended search. If you have the qualified staff and good research tools, you might consider offering some of these fee-based research services:

   extended subject and author searches of the literature and the Internet
   compilation of special bibliographies and reading lists
   literature reviews
   acquisition of out-of-print and collector items for private collections
   appraisal of antique books
   biographical research/obituaries
   trademark and patent searches
   advice on setting up corporate and private libraries
   cataloging private collections

assistance in preparing grants and proposals

teaching on-site or off-site courses

identification of old photos

finding magazine and news articles

compiling company, market, and industry profiles

compiling country profiles, news, financials, and rankings

industry trends or outlooks

competitive intelligence

financial statistics and data

legislative histories

demographic statistics

maps and travel information

market research

international trade information

government information

fact checking

historical statistics

information on art, history, or literature

genealogical research

With the exception of teaching off-site courses, virtually all these tasks can be done in most public libraries using available reference materials and the Internet. This work can also be performed after hours by moonlighting library staff who volunteer for paid overtime and who can be compensated with cash or compensatory time off at a later date. Charges for this type of work usually range from $30 to $125 per hour plus expenses. A rather well-developed model for fee-based public library services is the New York Public Library's NYPL Express (http://www.nypl.org/express/), which offers both research and document delivery.

In some areas, public libraries have set up research partnerships with their business communities via "corporate memberships" in partnership with business associations or chambers of commerce. A typical model is that of the James J. Hill Reference Library in St. Paul, Minnesota (www.hillsearch.org), where businesses or researchers take out "memberships" at $49.95 per month or $595 per year entitling them to special services including research seminars, subscription database access, and contract research.

If you decide to offer fee-based services, work with your board and solicitor to develop a guiding policy and model contract. On all research assignments, it is advisable to obtain agreement by both the client and the library on the assignment's details in advance of any work via a written letter contract covering engagement scope, staffing, fees, cost ceiling, and schedule. This will avoid misunderstandings and protect the library. (Sample library research agreements can be found in appendix F.)

Book and Calendar Publishing

Public libraries often produce and sell publications or original calendars either as byproducts of a program event, to commemorate a special occasion, or just to raise funds. Examples may include cookbooks containing either donated recipes or those from library-sponsored tasting or cooking contests, author lecture/book signings, book fairs, original photo books or calendars showing local historical sights, and collected works from library art or poetry classes or contests. For example, to commemorate our new library building's fifth anniversary, the library Friends group held a pet photo contest with the twelve winning pictures being compiled into a calendar, which was printed and sold in the library bookstore. The contest was also a fund-raising technique, because patrons were invited to vote for their favorite pet photos by placing dimes in cans in front of each candidate picture in a lobby display. The twelve photos with the most money were the winners. The calendar project yielded over $2,000 in income.

Selling Food and Drink

Prompted by the popularity of bookstore cafés, a number of libraries have begun offering refreshments for sale. This can range from a simple self-service table with an honor pay system in the lobby offering only a samovar of coffee and a plate of cookies to a Starbucks-like coffee shop serving latte and biscotti. Both approaches can generate income and patron satisfaction. A library in my area makes $200 per month with the coffee urn and homemade cookies, and the Ferguson Library in Stamford grosses over $100,000 with its upscale café. I know of another library that sells takeout popcorn, candy, and soft drinks to patrons borrowing videos as both a service and an income source.

Consider also setting up volunteer-run food stands in conjunction with major events sponsored by the library (see chapter 5). This can be as simple as selling soft drinks, donuts, and coffee or can be expanded to sell hot dogs, barbecue, sandwiches, soups, and pastries. We find that we can get local merchants or members of our Friends group to donate much of the food for our stands. Another alternative is to invite a vendor to set up a food trailer at your event, with a portion of the sales being donated to the library. Event food sales usually generate $500 or more surplus for our library.

Online Information Sources on Library Fund-Raising

In addition to the books on library fund-raising cited in the bibliography, here are a number of websites that address the topic:

- WebJunction: http://www.webjunction.org/do/LearningCenter?method=get CourseDetails&courseId=546
- American Library Association: http://www.ala.org/ala/alalibrary/libraryfact sheet/alalibraryfactsheet24.cfm]
- Library Administration and Management Association: http://www.ala.org/ala/ lama/lamacomunity/lamacommunities/fundraisingb/fundraisingfinancial.htm
- Association of Research Libraries: http://www.arl.org/pubscat/pubs/fundraising/ fund_intro.html
- TechSoup: http://www.techsoup.org/learningcenter/funding/index.cfm
- Friends of Libraries: http://www.folusa.org/sharing/fundraising.php
- Library Support Staff: http://www.librarysupportstaff.com/find$.html

As with most library activities, fund-raising should be governed by an appropriate policy. Stephanie Gerding gives good advice on how to develop such a policy in her recent article "Library Fund-Raising and Gift Policies."[3]

NOTES

1. Adrienne Chute and others, *Public Libraries in the United States: Fiscal Year 2004* (Washington, DC: National Center for Education Statistics, 2006).
2. Ibid.
3. Stephanie K. Gerding, "Library Fund-Raising and Gift Policies," *Public Libraries* 45, no. 5 (October 2006): 272–274.

CHAPTER FIVE

EARNING MONEY THROUGH BENEFIT EVENTS

Benefit events are the major fund-raisers for many public libraries. They also attract community attention and participation. As opposed to regular library programs, which may or may not generate income, these special events are organized for the primary purpose of raising money. After several years, benefit events can become community traditions, which build library support and recognition. Normally, most of the effort in staging benefit events is provided by library volunteers as opposed to paid library staff. Typical public library fund-raising events include the following:

1. Book sales
2. Auctions
3. Antique appraisal fairs
4. Flea markets
5. Theme parties and dinners
6. Bake sales
7. Art shows and sales
8. Fashion shows
9. Sporting events
10. Tours, tastings, and walks
11. Fee-based courses

Each of these types of events is discussed in detail below.

Book Sales

One of the most traditional of public library benefit events is the annual book sale. These are usually conducted by library volunteers and may be held either at the library or off-site at a school gymnasium, church, country club, or any other large, open facility rented for the purpose. Inventory for the book sale comes both from withdrawn library materials and from donations and includes books, periodicals, and AV materials. The book sale can run for one or several days, depending on the volume of materials to be sold. Preparation for a library book sale involves several tasks, which may need to begin up to a year in advance. These tasks include the following:

1. Recruiting book sale chair and volunteers
2. Receipt, sorting, and storage of inventory
3. Pricing of inventory
4. Reserving a sale venue
5. Promoting the sale
6. Obtaining sufficient sales tables
7. Transporting inventory to the sale site
8. Laying out materials to be sold
9. Sales and cleanup
10. Obtaining bags and cartons for purchases
11. Arranging for ancillary sale items
12. Disposition of unsold items

Our library starts planning for the annual spring book sale a year in advance. As is typically the case with many public libraries, our Friends of the Library manage our book sale. Their first step is to appoint a book sale chairperson, who is often the president of the Friends group. The book sale chairperson will then recruit a committee whose size is determined by the scope of the sale and the number of tasks. Although many people will not be needed until the time of the sale, the critical advance tasks of soliciting and sorting book donations and generating publicity should be staffed as soon as possible. As donations are received, they are boxed using surplus banana boxes obtained from supermarkets and are then transported to a barn we rent as a warehouse. It helps here to have a volunteer or staff member with a pickup truck. At the warehouse, books are removed from the boxes, sorted by type, genre, and audience (e.g., fiction, reference, gardening, children, audio books, films, music recordings, etc.), priced, and reboxed by category with the cartons marked as to contents. Collector books are priced by value, others by the piece, and mass-market paperbacks and old magazines are sold by the bag. Try to perform the sorting and price-labeling tasks as books are received, rather than waiting until just before the book sale, to ensure efficiency.

We do not have enough room at the library to hold our two-day book sale there, so we rent a gymnasium at a nearby church school for the event. We like it there because of its layout and amenities. It is easy to unload our books there, the church provides the tables we need, there is a large lobby where we can set up a cashier's table, and they let us use an adjacent cafeteria and kitchen for our food stand. Other libraries hold their book sales at golf clubs, firehouses, or Veterans of Foreign Wars halls. Wherever you hold yours, make sure to rent the facility for at least the two days before the sale to allow time for delivering the books from storage and laying them out on tables in the proper categories with the right pricing and genre signs.

Starting about three months prior to our sale, we start advertising locally to encourage book donations, and we also advertise the sale nationally to the antique book trade. Antique and out-of-print book dealers are big buyers who purchase to build their inventories and to satisfy their "want" lists. Therefore, we try to manage the timing of our book sale to be immediately before or after the book sale of the largest library in our county, so that out-of-town book dealers can visit both sales in a single trip. You can advertise your book sale nationally by listing it on both the Book Scout (www.booksalescout.com) and Book Sale Finder (www.booksalefinder.com) websites, which list library book sales by state. Listing is free.

We typically offer about 40,000 items at our book sale, and it takes our volunteer team about two days to transport them to the sale site and lay them out on tables by type, along with genre and pricing signs. Make sure you line up enough people, supplies, furniture, and vehicles to get this done efficiently. We obtain about 1,000 used or new grocery bags and cartons from both the community and supermarkets to be used by book buyers to cart home their bargains. You should obtain cash boxes or cash registers for your cashiers and a supply of small bills and coins to make change for early purchasers. Arrange for your treasurer or bookkeeper to regularly collect and deposit the sales proceeds to avoid too much cash accumulation. Also ensure that your food stand and memento table (if you opt to have them) are stocked adequately and staffed during the entire sale. It is a good idea to assign an experienced person as a "floor boss" for each shift to troubleshoot and oversee that everything goes smoothly.

Finally, decide in advance of the sale what you will do with any unsold items that may remain. You can box them for storage at your warehouse until next year or arrange for a bulk publications broker to buy them "as is/where is" by the truckload at salvage prices. This may not yield a great deal of cash, but it avoids a lot of aggravation and gets rid of unpopular stock. As a last step, we bring in a volunteer cleanup crew to fold the tables and put the gym back the way we found it. Scout troops and service clubs are great for this task if you can recruit them.

You can see that a book sale requires a lot of planning and work, but it can yield good results. Our small library's annual book sale generates a $10,000–$15,000 surplus each year. The annual book sale of the largest library in our county exceeds $200,000 in revenue.

Auctions

Benefit auctions are not yet as popular as book sales among small public libraries, but they can be just as lucrative as fund-raisers and less physically labor-intensive. Auctions, however, require skillful advanced planning, promotion, and execution, and most important, a skilled auctioneer.

In planning a benefit auction, the very first step is to find a professional (or a very skilled amateur) auctioneer who is willing to advise you on planning and help run your sale, hopefully on a pro bono basis. This is not as hard as it may seem, because there are many local auctioneers who are willing to donate their skills to worthy not-for-profits both as a community service and to increase their exposure in a very competitive marketplace. Try both ends of the auctioneer spectrum first, the young guys and gals just starting out and the established old-timers. The young folks may want to build a reputation, and the old-timers may want to give back to the community.

My library hooked up with a young man in his thirties who was interested in building a following, and he pledged to be our pro bono auctioneer for as long as he remained in the business. As a fringe benefit he lends us 200 chairs and portable roadside signs, brings along his computerized auction accounting system, and donates all the auction bidder number cards and receipts we need. We gratefully acknowledge his support via our newsletter, press releases, and letters of thanks. Therefore, if you can establish a long-term relationship with an auctioneer, you are well on your way to ensuring your benefit auction's success.

When starting a benefit auction, learn from others who have done it before. If you know of another institution that conducts a benefit auction, contact its auction chairperson and ask if he or she will share their experience and knowledge with you. When my library first decided to have a benefit auction, I sought out the auction chair of another small public library that had held an annual benefit auction for a number of years. The chairperson graciously shared her experience, forms, and lists with me and even invited me to be an inside observer at their next auction. The knowledge I gained in this way shortened our learning time and helped us avoid many errors in planning our first auction.

Planning for a benefit auction should begin at least six months before the set auction date. The planning and implementation steps include the following:

1. Recruiting an auction chair and volunteer committee
2. Selecting an auction date
3. Selecting an auction site
4. Gathering auction equipment and supplies
5. Storing auction items
6. Defining the scope of goods and services to be solicited
7. Defining the auction promotion plan and materials
8. Design and scope of the auction catalog
9. Design and creation of donor-solicitation flyers and literature
10. Design and creation of posters and banners
11. Developing and classifying donor prospect solicitation lists
12. Assigning solicitation "territories" to solicitors
13. Direct mailing of solicitation letters
14. Field soliciting
15. Pickup, delivery, and receipt of solicited items
16. Cataloging, sorting, and storing donated materials by type

17. Donor acknowledgment
18. Promoting the sale
19. Obtaining necessary public sale licenses and permissions
20. Transporting inventory to sale site
21. Obtaining auction paperwork, records, accounting, and sales receipt system
22. Auction preview
23. Auction day staffing
24. Auction
25. Ancillary sale activities
26. Disposition of unsold items

Many of the planning and implementation steps for a benefit auction are treated in detail below.

Recruiting an Auction Chair and Volunteer Committee

A successful auction committee requires people with special skills. Correctly staffing your benefit auction is therefore critical. Recruit your auction chairperson carefully because she must function as a combination of huckster and maestro. The chairperson must conduct a team of solicitors, merchandise managers, catalogers, auctioneers, auction clerks, and runners. She must also manage auction logistics and promotion and must ensure that everything comes together in harmony on the day of the auction. I have found that people with sales management and marketing backgrounds make good auction chairpersons. In my mind, an essential skill for the auction chair and solicitors is chutzpah, a lack of inhibition in asking people for donations and refusing to take no for an answer. If you want some really nice and unusual donations (e.g., an auto, a weekend at a vacation home, five minutes of free shopping at the supermarket, a ride with the police chief, lunch with the mayor, etc.), it helps to employ solicitors who are well known and respected in the community.

In addition to a chairperson and field, telephone, and mail solicitors, a good auction team should also include one or more merchandise managers to log in, catalog, and store donated goods and services. Also critical are advertising or publication specialists to generate promotional flyers, posters, and auction catalogs and to sell advertising in the catalog. You should also designate a database manager to maintain and update computer files of prospects, donors, and donations. For the auction day and preview, you will need auction preview monitors, sales clerks, auction runners, cashiers, and food stand managers.

Selecting an Auction Date

Selecting the optimum date for your auction requires balancing several factors. You will have to verify that your auctioneer is available to preside over the event. Then make sure the site is available. Ensure that your auction helpers will be available. You should also check event calendars for your area to avoid competing with another auction or event on the same day. Further, pick a date when potential bidders will be in town. For example, do not schedule an auction over a holiday weekend when everyone is away at the shore or mountains, as this will really hurt your bottom line. When selecting a date it is good to also specify the dates of the auction preview (e.g., the two days and morning preceding the auction) and the time and duration of the auction. We hold our auction on a Saturday in August, with preview and sign-up from 8:00 a.m. to 10:00 a.m., and bidding starting at 10:00 a.m. and concluding between 1:00 and 2:00 p.m. These hours also help sales at our food stand, which serves both breakfast and lunch. We have learned to schedule the auctioning of the highlight big-ticket items, such as autos or vacation trips, at midday when audience attendance peaks.

Selecting an Auction Site

Selecting an auction site requires consideration of your audience and objectives. There are three basic options:

- on-site at the library
- off-site at a church, school, golf club, and so on
- off-site at a restaurant banquet hall

You can conduct your auction within the library (if you have the room) or in a rented tent on the library's lawn (assuming you hold your auction in warm weather). The tent and folding chairs can be set up the day before the auction by the rental company team. We select a tent with side flaps that can be rolled down in the event of rain. We selected the on-site option at the suggestion of our auctioneer, who advised that people tend to bid higher at benefit auctions when the auction is held on the premises of the recipient institution. Moreover, holding an auction in a big yellow tent creates a party-like atmosphere where everyone lightens up and has a good time.

If your library has limited space or your auction occurs during a period of inclement weather, then holding it off-site is the only option. I have seen successful auctions held in school gyms, restaurants, firehouses, armories, country clubs, and churches. Our auctioneer, however, cautions against holding a library auction at another charitable institution's site (e.g., church), lest the public get confused as to which institution receives the proceeds. He advises that an auction always generates more cash if held at the beneficiary's site.

I know of several institutions (including public libraries) that hold a combined benefit auction and banquet in a nice restaurant (or catered at the library as an option). Purchasing a ticket for the banquet (at twenty dollars or more per couple) also gets you an auction bidder's number. At the end of the meal, diners remain at their tables and the auction proceeds at the center of the banquet hall. A combined auction/banquet event hosted by another small public library in my region has become an important social event where groups of friends reserve tables in advance and then compete with each other in the bidding. Now in its ninth year, this small library auction/banquet yields about $60,000 each year!

Gathering Auction Equipment and Supplies

An auction requires that a certain amount of equipment and supplies be ordered in advance, with much of it not needed until auction day. This includes the tent, chairs, auction podium, stage, sound system, preview display tables, cashier computers and registers with appropriate software, bidder number cards, bidder receipts, signage and banners, silent auction and raffle materials, gift certificate forms, auction letterhead stationary, solicitation forms, and donation receipts. The auction chairperson should start making a list of needed items with dates needed early and should run it by the experienced auctioneer to ensure that nothing critical is omitted. Do not be bashful about asking other institutions that conduct auctions to share their "do lists" with you.

Storing Auction Items

Arrange for a library staff member or volunteer with a truck or van to pick up donated items from donors on request. As your soliciting proceeds, you will find donations coming in and beginning to pile up. Some of these may be quite large (e.g., bicycles, exercise equipment, office chairs, etc.) and you may begin to run out of storage space in your small library. Therefore, you may need to arrange for an off-site storage site for about six months. You can rent one, or you may be able to obtain a pro bono storage site in return for favorable mention or a free ad in your auction catalog. We usually find a local self-storage locker vendor who will lend us an unused locker for up to six months. One of these garage-sized lockers is usually sufficient to hold all of our auction donations with the exception of automobiles, which we store in the library parking lot with a sign advertising, "You can bid on this car at our forthcoming auction."

Defining the Scope of Goods and Services to Be Solicited

Experience has shown us that it is advisable to establish limits on what the library will solicit and accept for its auction. This helps both to focus solicitors and to avoid getting items that are difficult or impossible to auction off. At our first annual auction, we had no restrictions and, to be honest, we ended up with some real junk that we could not sell. We also received a lot of small items that were eventually sold, but really slowed things down and made the auction too long.

We solicit both services and goods as auction donations. Among "services" we include work sessions, instruction, and professional or consulting services donated by tradespeople, artisans, doctors, therapists, lawyers, landscapers, sculptors, plumbers, photographers, carpenters, and investment advisors. Also included among service donations are gift certificates from restaurants, bed and breakfasts, hotels, and other retailers. One prized auction donation is a certificate from a local supermarket good for five minutes of free shopping. This can sell for $1,000.

Interesting services that can be solicited from members of the community include the donation of time at a vacation property, a cruise on a yacht (or a canoe), and special instruction in a craft or sport. A number of community members have donated custom catering services to our auction where they deliver a meal or baked goods to the successful bidder at a mutually agreed-upon time and place. For example, for the last two years, one woman has donated a high tea for eight at the winning bidder's home, and another will deliver a home-baked pastry treat of the month to the winner. We also solicit services from government officials, politicians, and media personalities. This has yielded such interesting auction donations as a ride in the police chief's cruiser, lunch with the mayor, a guided tour of Washington, DC, with lunch in the Senate dining room from our U.S. senator, a tour of the state capital with lunch from our state senator, and a guided tour of the local TV station with the news anchor person. These "tour" services frequently receive bids of up to $500. Keep an open mind and you may get some cool items.

Try to acquire one or more big-ticket items for your auction, because these can be major draws as well as money- and publicity makers. These can include vehicles, boats, vacation trips, or farm equipment. In this regard, my library is fortunate in having a local used car dealer agree to donate a "cream puff" vehicle worth at least $5,000 to our auction each year. Two weeks before the auction, the dealer delivers three "candidate" cars (i.e., a convertible, a sedan, and a station wagon) to display in our library parking lot, and the winning bidder takes his or her choice.

Experience has taught us to become more selective in the auction goods we accept. At our first auction, it appeared that a number of people cleaned out their attics and sheds when they delivered to us boxes full of dusty and musty-smelling old toys, dirty appliances, rusty tools, and used clothing that needed lots of cleanup and yielded few bids. Others donated old refrigerators, gas ranges, and used furniture that we could not sell and had to trash. Obsolete computer hardware, we also learned, does not sell and costs money to dispose of. We therefore now focus on new or like-new merchandise and no longer accept used appliances, used clothing, old toys, large pieces of furniture, or computer hardware more than three years old. The only exceptions are bona fide antiques and collectibles. We accept used automobiles only on the condition that they can pass a state inspection.

Even with these selective criteria, we try to keep an open mind when we are offered something unusual or "interesting." For example, at our first auction someone donated a cast-iron manhole cover weighing about a hundred pounds and labeled "Mount Joy, PA Sewer Authority." My staff berated me for accepting it, but it sold for $70 and yielded a lot of laughs. This year our local borough's maintenance department donated three manhole covers, two fire hydrants, an old parking meter, and a few old street signs which were auctioned off, yielding bids of $50 to $100 each and a great deal of wisecracks and fun. The unique (or perhaps weird) nature of these items even attracted media attention, and they were highlighted in a half-page newspaper feature story.

Creating Auction Promotional Materials

The auction promotion team will need to plan, design, and produce several types of promotional pieces. These include public solicitation flyers, business donation and sponsorship solicitation letters, posters, banners, newspapers ads, press releases, gift certificates, and the auction catalog and sponsorship ads in that catalog.

We produce two types of solicitation flyers, a generic one and one for vehicles. The generic one states "Please Donate Something to Our Auction," gives the auction date, summarizes the auction's purpose and the types of goods and services we seek, provides instructions for donors, and includes a tear-off donor reply slip. The vehicle flyer leads off with the statement "You Have an Alternative to Selling This Vehicle. You Can Donate It to the Library and Take a Tax Deduction." Its content is similar to the generic flyer. We print both flyers on colored paper to attract attention. The generic flyer is given to library patrons and left with potential donors who are visited by auction solicitors. We place the vehicle flyer on roadside vehicles that are for sale and have obtained two cars in this manner.

Business solicitation letters provide potential donors with the option of donating a good or service or sponsoring an advertisement in the auction catalog. Sample ad formats and a reply card are also included. Sponsor ads come in different sizes and range in price from $25 to $500. These catalog ads are popular with business professionals and tradespeople such as doctors, real estate agents, and plumbers.

We experimented with direct mail promotion of our auction by mailing postcards to 8,000 library patrons. We found that this did not increase attendance at the sale, so we discontinued the practice.

It is useful to produce posters announcing the auction, which can be placed on bulletin boards throughout the community. We also hang a fifteen-foot-long auction banner between two telephone poles over our town's main street two weeks prior to our auction (with proper utility company and municipal permissions). Running ads announcing the auction in local weekly newspapers during the three weeks prior to the auction also serves to draw bidders. We also send auction press releases to the media and the cable TV channel's community bulletin board a month before the auction.

It is our standard practice to provide each auction attendee with a catalog listing the items that will be auctioned and acknowledging their donors. Over the years we've expanded ours from a few stapled sheets into a thirty-page, saddle-stitched, bound booklet which also contains sponsored advertisements ranging in size from a business card ($25) to a full page ($500). Sponsored ads give businesses and individuals who may not be able to donate an auction good or service an opportunity to show their support for your event. These ads generate about $3,000 per auction. The auction catalog is also a good place to acknowledge and thank your auction committee and others who have worked on the auction.

Auction Soliciting

The auction field solicitor team will need to start work about six months before the sale on a number of key tasks. Start by developing a list of prospective donors broken down by businesses and individuals. Then decide on the mode of contact: face-to-face, telephone, or mail. The list of organizations and individuals to be visited should then be sorted by geographic location and business type before being assigned to field solicitors. For purposes of efficiency, it is useful to assign similar prospects (e.g., auto dealers) to the same person and to group geographically adjacent prospects together to minimize travel. As with direct funds soliciting, face-to-face and telephone auction solicitors will need to be trained using appropriate scripts. We also find it helps to provide field solicitors with distinctive name tags or T-shirts identifying them as representatives of the public library.

If a field solicitor's visit or phone call does not yield an immediate donation or sponsorship, leave or send a solicitation flyer and then follow up with a repeat phone call or visit in about two weeks. You should also follow up on solicitation letters with a phone call within two weeks. To assist donors, offer to pick up any donated items at the donor's convenience and provide receipts. If the donation is a service, offer to generate a gift certificate if the donor does not have one available. Software packages, such as PrintMaster, allow you to easily create handsome certificates.

Cataloging, Sorting, and Storing Donated Materials by Type

To stay ahead of the tide, items should be cataloged and entered into the auction database as they are received. Descriptive cataloging should include a description of item, brand name if applicable, estimated value, and donor name, address, and phone number. With the exception of estimated value and donor address and number, all these data elements will appear in the auction catalog, unless the donor wants to remain anonymous. Assigning item numbers and type of donation classification codes is optional, but if you do it, do it as the item is received. Ours is an "absolute" auction with no "reserve" or minimum bids. Therefore, although we ask donors to indicate the value of their gift, we do not allow them to set a minimum price for the item. It is your option to decide if you wish to establish minimum "reserve" prices. Our auctioneer advises us not to specify the estimated value of an auction item in its catalog listing because he feels it limits the bidding.

Donor Acknowledgment

Rather than waiting until all donations are in, we cite donors in our newspaper ads and library posters on a regular basis prior to the auction, because we believe that this encourages additional donations. However, all donors should be listed in the auction catalog. We also send each donor a thank-you letter. Because we print our auction catalog a week prior to the auction, we run off an addendum on auction day to acknowledge any last-minute donations.

Obtaining Necessary Public Sale Licenses and Permissions

In many communities, a license may be required for a public auction sale, although this may be waived for a not-for-profit library. You may also need a permit to erect a tent, hang a banner across a thoroughfare, or operate a food stand. Check with your local authorities to ensure that you do not violate any laws.

Transporting Inventory to Sale Site

If you have stored your auction inventory away from the auction preview site, it will be necessary to arrange for people and equipment to move it. In addition to drafting volunteers and staff with strong backs (whom my father used to call "schleppers"), it is helpful to have at your disposal a pickup truck or large van, mover's dollies, cartons, and padding for breakable items. If you keep these items handy on auction day, you can use them to help buyers load and carry home their treasures.

Obtaining Auction Paperwork, Records, Accounting, and Sales Receipt System

A typical auction requires a certain amount of paperwork, including

- bidder registration forms
- bidder number cards
- list of items purchased by bidder with total cost
- proxy bid forms
- sales receipt forms

A system to keep track of who has bought what and at what price will be needed as the auction progresses. This can be either a manual or computer-based system where an auction clerk maintains an ongoing ledger record of each sale showing the bidder number, item purchases, and purchase price.

If you employ a professional auctioneer, it is probably that he will already have all the paperwork and record-keeping systems necessary, and perhaps he can donate or lend these to you for your auction. Our library's pro bono auctioneer not only donates the paper forms and lends us his computer system, but even brings along an auction clerk to record each sale.

Auction Preview

Though not absolutely necessary, conducting an auction preview will usually help auction sales. If a preview is to be held, advertise it in advance. Typically, a preview involves laying out all of the items to be auctioned a day or two in advance of the auction for inspection by potential bidders. To expedite auction day logistics, hold the preview at the auction venue and lay the items out in the order they are to be auctioned so they can go directly from the preview table to the auction block. Recruit and assign auction preview staff to monitor the preview room, provide catalogs, and take proxy bids from people who cannot attend the auction or choose not to bid for themselves.

Auction Day Staffing

To ensure a smooth-flowing auction, you will need adequate auction day staffing. For a typical library auction, this will include one or more auctioneers; an auction clerk to record sales; runners to bring out goods to be auctioned; a spotter or two to both help the auctioneer spot bidders and deliver sold goods; two cashiers to issue bidder number cards, tally totals, collect payments, and issue receipts; and, finally, a cleanup crew. You will also need people to handle any ancillary activities you set up.

Ancillary Sale Activities

Auction ancillary activities can include a silent auction, food stand, and a raffle or memento sale table. A silent auction is where people write in bids for certain displayed items which will not be sold at the regular auction. The highest write-in bid gets the item. The selling of raffle tickets for gift baskets is also found at many auctions. A food stand or a banquet is often an adjunct to a benefit auction. If managed properly, these supplemental activities can add $1,000 or more to your auction take. In my library's case, we have found the food stand to be profitable but have had only marginal results with the silent auction and raffle. Our Friends group also always manages to sell a fair share of library mementos at our auction.

Disposition of Unsold Items

Alas, you may find that not every one of the treasures donated to your auction has attracted a buyer. Therefore, you may want to make some arrangement for the disposition of leftover merchandise in advance of the auction. As options you can consider donating them to a not-for-profit thrift shop, selling (or just giving) them to a local salvage dealer (aka "junkman"), or just transporting them to the local dump. If you donate or give your leftover items to a salvage service, try to get them to pick up the items at the library immediately after the auction to avoid the bother of storing and transporting them.

Auction Financial Benefits

Although it involves a lot of work, a library benefit auction can be a real money-maker. We held our first library benefit auction, with some trepidation, in 2002. To assuage our concerns, our experienced auctioneer assured us that we would gross at least $8,000. We actually broke $10,000, and at our fourth annual auction in 2006, we approached $15,000 in sales. After expenses, we netted about $12,000. As cited earlier, a small public library in our county holds a midwinter combined auction and banquet and grosses nearly $60,000.

Antique Appraisal Fairs

Patterned after the popular *Antiques Roadshow* public television program, library-sponsored antique appraisal fairs can be fun as well as good fund-raisers. This type of event can be held either at the library or off-site at a school gym or rented hall. Canvass local antique dealers and appraisers in order to locate four or five who would be willing to donate their services to your event. Pick a date, advertise, and sell tickets in advance.

We hold our event on a Saturday from 9:00 a.m. to 4:00 p.m. We sell tickets at $5 per item to be appraised or three for $12. To ensure a smooth flow at the appraisal fair, we designate appraisers by their specialties (e.g., jewelry, furniture, porcelain, art, etc.) and schedule appraisals by the hour. When a patron arrives at the designated hour with the item to be appraised, a volunteer triage officer directs the patron to the table of the relevant specialty appraiser.

With advance advertising, an antique appraisal fair can bring out 500 to 1,000 people and gross up to $5,000. An ancillary food stand can add $500–$1,000 to the take.

Flea Markets

If your library has a fairly large parking lot, you can put it to good fund-raising use by holding a weekend flea market there. We have done this on holiday weekends, where we rent each parking space to a vendor for the day for a fee of fifteen dollars. Volunteers do the sign-ups and sale day ushering, so your only real out-of-pocket expense will be advertising and promotion. To add to your take, set up an ancillary food stand and a library Friends table selling surplus books, mementos, and baked goods. A word of advice is to promote the flea market as "rain or shine" and collect vendor fees in advance. That way, you will be able to cover your expenses even if it rains and, believe it or not, some vendors will set up under awnings and some die-hard bargain hunters will come even if it pours!

Theme Parties and Dinners

You can have a lot of fun, encourage reading, and even make a few bucks by having a library-sponsored literary theme party or dinner. Have people come in costume representing their favorite literary characters. Possible fiction themes are romance, horror, war, adventure, western, mystery, and so on. You can also have a nonfiction theme, such as science or current affairs. Try naming your food dishes in keeping with the theme.

For example, to celebrate the centennial of Einstein's theory of relativity, our library held an Einstein Science Trivia Party. We drafted a middle-school science teacher as our master of ceremonies and dressed him as Einstein. Patrons were invited to form teams and compete in a science trivia contest. Seven teams, representing several families, a supermarket, and the post office, competed for science-oriented prizes. The post office team, who borrowed and read a bunch of popular physics books in preparation, won the contest, proving that reading pays off. We served such dishes as nuclear subs, pumpkin π, photon fruit dip, pulsar potato chips, e=m(e)clairs, and plasma pretzels. You can have fun and let both your culinary and literary imaginations flow as you come up with some interesting theme dishes such as Sherlock Holmes's hot dogs, Casanova's casserole, Dan's *Brown*ies, John's Gris*ham*, Deepak Chopra's liver, David Baldacci's focaccia, Stephen King's knishes, and Shakespeare's shish kabob.

Bake Sales

The bake sale is a very traditional fund-raiser for not-for-profits. It does not make a great deal of money, but it is simple, effective, and, alas, fattening.

Very simply, you set a date, encourage your volunteers and staff to donate home-made baked goods, advertise, and hold the sale. We actually do this throughout the year by soliciting donated baked goods for our book sale, auction, and flea market food stands. We also solicit and auction off baskets of baked goods at our benefit auction, where a cake or pie baked by a well-known resident can generate bids of up to $100 from her friends and family.

Art Shows and Sales

Try teaming up with local artists, or even better a local artists association or craft guild, and hold an art show and sale at the library. It's a fun event, it encourages and supports your local art community, and it can generate some income for the library.

Rather than charge admission or an artist exhibition fee, we take a 20–30 percent commission on any sales made at the event and let the artists price their wares accordingly. To earn its fee and facilitate accounting, the library can provide a central volunteer-run cashier service to collect sale payments, package sold items, keep tabs on all sales by artist and piece, and distribute sales reports and proceeds to exhibitors at the event's conclusion. As a byproduct, you can ask the artists to continue the relationship by giving you works of art to sell on a consignment basis at your library bookstore. Again, a refreshment stand may generate some additional income, and you can even get classy and serve wine and cheese (if your library's bylaws do not prohibit alcohol).

Fashion Shows

You can invite local boutiques and couturiers to hold a benefit fashion show at your library. You can charge a modest admission fee and ask the vendors for a donation in return or a percentage of any sales resulting from the event.

Sporting Events

The library can sponsor a benefit sporting event such as a golf tournament at a local country club, a bicycle race, a runners' marathon, a boat race, and so on. Income can be derived both from admission fees and from having local businesses and residents donate cash and goods as prizes, with any surplus going to the library. If you have a professional or minor league team in your area, sponsor a sports night out at the local arena or stadium.

We did that in 2006 in cooperation with the municipality and chamber of commerce. The local minor league baseball team provided a block of 250 tickets to us at half price, which we sold in the library at full price. At the game, our library was highlighted on the digital scoreboard and I was even invited to throw out the first ball!

Tours, Tastings, and Walks

You can work with your community to sponsor or cosponsor a town-wide event where your library shares in the proceeds. It could be a walking tour or open house day event where historic, interesting, or unusual homes, buildings, and sites open their doors to allow visitors to tour the facilities. A tasting tour can involve visiting interesting eateries and sampling their wares. Vendors donate their services, you sell tickets in advance, and the sponsors split the proceeds.

As an example, a town in my area, which is home to a chocolate factory and several upmarket candy stores, sponsors an annual Chocolate Walk in which ticket holders visit the chocolate works and stores and get samples to taste at each stop. A riverfront town with a rather romantic history sponsors an annual Halloween Ghost Walk (costumes optional) in which historic "haunted houses" are visited and costumed guides introduce visitors to the resident spooks.

Fee-Based Courses

Although a library's educational programs are not necessarily established to raise funds, a public library is justified in charging modest fees for the courses it conducts. This is especially true if the course involves consumable materials or a paid instructor.

For example, at the request of parents, my library initiated group classes and workshops for homeschooled children in such subjects as science, art, home economics, computers, and language. We normally impose charges of up to twenty-five dollars per student to pay for expendable materials and instructors. For adults, we host a monthly Culture and Cooking event in which we invite community members born in foreign countries to share their birth nation's culture and national dishes with their neighbors. Since we reimburse the presenters for the cost of the food ingredients, we suggest a two-dollar "donation" from each attendee.

However, in charging use some discretion. Gauge your audience carefully and do not impose attendance fees if these discourage your target audience from participating. As an alternative, you can follow the custom of some churches and, rather than imposing a mandatory admission fee, suggest a freewill offering from event attendees. If you do impose an event fee, it is a good idea to advertise it in advance in order to avoid conflict or embarrassment at the event.

The next chapter will address obtaining support for your library from the community in forms other than cash.

CHAPTER SIX

OBTAINING NONCASH SUPPORT
FROM THE COMMUNITY

In seeking the resources to keep your library functioning, and even flourishing, do not overlook donations of services and goods, because these can often be as good as or, in some cases, even better than cash. This type of support can come in two forms: (1) bartering and partnering and (2) gift in-kind donations.

Bartering and Partnering

An oft-overlooked mode of obtaining needed resources is bartering the use of library facilities or services for services or goods from local entrepreneurs or organizations. We have let businesses and associations use our facilities and rather than charging a rental fee, we have received valuable services in return. For example, when local business people inquire about renting our meeting room, we offer them the option of providing the library with goods or services in lieu of cash. In another instance, we allow a high school club to use our library parking lot for an event, and in return, the energetic teenagers from the club (along with their adult leader) volunteer to staff several library activities.

Conducting a joint program with another organization or business is another mode of successful partnering, which can help to stretch limited library resources. Consider joint programs and fund-raisers with other libraries, groups, and businesses. As an example, we allowed the local chamber of commerce to combine its annual chicken barbecue with our library's annual benefit auction. In return, they share their income with the library. Check with local businesses to see if they could have a "benefit afternoon" in which a portion of their sales during that period will be turned over to your library. This has been done in my area by a dairy, a deli, and a Mexican fast-food shop. A book sale in partnership with a school is another traditional mode of library fund-raising.

You can find more on using partnering as a means of creating innovative library programs in chapter 9.

Gift in-Kind Donations

A public library can solicit gifts in kind of goods or services for either its own use or for resale to generate cash. In addition to items for its collections and book sale, the library can seek surplus equipment, food for program events, office furniture, printing services and copy paper from print shops, vehicles for its own use or to auction, servicing of library vehicles, warehouse storage space, and even original artwork to decorate the library and for resale. As an example of the value of gifts in kind, we were able to establish a computer-learning laboratory in our library through a gift of ten surplus computers from the local Blue Shield medical insurance carrier.

To prevent any misunderstandings, discourage donors from imposing limitations on their gifts in kind. Whether it is a book or an automobile, donors should be made to understand that the library must reserve the right to keep or dispose of the item at its discretion.

You can also build your library's collections through selective solicitation of donations. Local authors and local publishers, such as historical societies, may be willing to donate copies of the reference and fiction books and periodicals that they publish to your library. In another mode, enthusiasts such as model railroaders, golfers, or investors may be willing to bankroll the acquisition of collection materials in their areas of interest. You don't have to limit your soliciting of collection materials to books. For example, I talked a toy-making firm into donating more than 100 preschool children's puzzles and toys to our library, which we now lend out to parents. We also have a high-tech reading magnifier machine donated by a local service club.

When you need professional or skilled assistance, seek pro bono labor from professional practices (e.g., lawyers, accountants, etc.) and skilled tradespeople (e.g., plumbers, landscapers, electricians, painters, etc.) in the community. This can be a valuable gift in kind to the public library. In addition, do not overlook the possibility of employing individuals required to perform community service or internships as library "volunteers" (see chapter 10).

Guidelines for Donations

I recommend that your library adopt a rule that all donations, regardless of value, must be acknowledged. This is necessary to both maintain the goodwill of your community and to encourage future donations. There are several ways to do this, including letters, bulletin boards, advertisements, newsletter lists, program lists, telephone calls, ceremonies, plaques, and dedication of areas or items.

Every cash or in-kind donation is important to its donor, as it is a very personal demonstration of support for your institution. At a minimum, acknowledge the donation with a letter of thanks. We record each donation we receive in a database using Giftworks software. At the end of the month, our community relations coordinator generates a thank-you letter from this file for each donor of cash or a gift in kind.

A thank-you letter from the president or secretary of the library's board of trustees acknowledges major donations of $100 or more. Each month a listing of the prior month's donors, classified by individuals and businesses, is posted on our library lobby's bulletin board. We cite the amount of the donations in the letters but not in a public notice. Monthly bulletin board notices are cumulated and also published in the library's quarterly newsletter. Some libraries group and report their donor acknowledgments by amount category (e.g., $100+ = silver; $500+ = gold; $1,000+ = platinum; $5,000+ = diamond, etc.). Donors who choose to be anonymous receive letters but are not publicly listed.

For donations to a special event such as a benefit auction, in addition to the acknowledgments cited in the previous paragraph, we also include a list of auction goods donors in the auction catalog and in both pre- and post-auction half-page newspaper advertisements that list and thank all donors. We have received favorable feedback (and increased donations) from this practice.

For particularly significant donations, in addition to the practices cited above, a personal telephone call from a library officer should be made. If all sides agree, a "photo op" ceremony can be held where the donor presents the check with the press invited to attend, photograph, and report the event. Significant gifts can also be commemorated with a plaque or by dedicating a portion of the library to the donor. My own library, the Milanof-Schock Library, is named after two donors, and each of our community rooms, our boardroom, and our kitchen is dedicated to the name of a significant library benefactor.

Finally, do not forget to acknowledge the donations of money and more important, effort, from your library's Friends group and volunteers. Consider sending these important human assets thank-you cards and token gifts. Cite them in your publications. Throw a thank-you party for them. Our library's staff does this in the form of an annual volunteer and Friends' potluck appreciation dinner to say thank you, and provides each volunteer with a memento gift. We also regularly cite the good work of volunteers and Friends in the library newsletter.

Make it a point to learn the names of all major donors so you can personally thank them for their support when they visit the library. A personal "thank you" and a smile can go a long way.

The next chapter will explore the use of grants as a means to fund library activities and projects.

CHAPTER SEVEN

GRANTSMANSHIP

The Art of Winning Grants

Grants can be a means of obtaining funding for special needs or special projects. This chapter will give you some pointers on pursuing grant funds for your small public library. (Additional sources of information on grants can be found in the bibliography.)

Although winning a grant may at first seem daunting to the uninitiated, it can be accomplished with a little effort and care. In three years, I was able to win more than $100,000 in grants for my small public library from both government and private sources. Grant winning requires first defining a clear set of needs for your library, finding relevant grant sources, and then applying a little imagination, a little common sense, some writing ability, and just following instructions.

A "grant" is really a formal donation of money, or if a grant in kind, of services or goods, usually earmarked for a specific purpose and in response to a formal request. Most grants are competitive, wherein several grant seekers compete for a limited amount of funds. There are also a few discretionary cash grants, which allow the library to use the cash as it desires; and occasionally noncompetitive grants are awarded for "good deeds" without a formal application being required. First, we will focus on how to win a competitive nondiscretionary grant.

Government agencies, private foundations, corporations, or individuals may award grants. Although application procedures and eligibility criteria may vary from grantor to grantor organization, the essential steps in grant seeking are basically the same. They consist of the following:

1. Finding a granting organization whose mission and scope match your needs
2. Obtaining the grant application package
3. Verifying your eligibility
4. Establishing the application writing and submission schedule
5. Preliminary research and fact-finding
6. Partnering
7. Preparing the application proposal
8. Following application outline discipline
9. Submitting the application proposal

Finding a Granting Organization Whose Mission and Scope Match Your Needs

Grants from Foundations and Individuals

Soliciting grants from foundations and individual philanthropists requires careful and focused thought and planning. I picked up a valuable insight on this at a recent not-for-profit fund-raising seminar: *foundations and philanthropists have a need to give and not-for-profit institutions have a need to receive.* Success lies in connecting these two needs.

Using your definition of your library's mission and goals (see chapter 3 on mission and goal definition), find a foundation or philanthropist whose charitable giving focus matches your library's mission and goals, and you will have a very good chance of success in getting a grant. Use your research skills and reference tools to find potential benefactors. Employ relevant directories, the Internet, local news media, and grantsmanship newsletters and databases as well as recommendations from knowledgeable advisors to identify potential donors who might be sympathetic toward public libraries in communities like yours. Make contacts among the local not-for-profit community to identify charitable events, receptions, and seminars that are attended by potential donors. Attend these get-togethers and "work the floor" to make personal contacts with those who can help your library.

Once you have identified a potential grant source, you can begin your grant application process. Analyze the granting organization's prior grant awards as to nature of grants, nature of recipients, amounts, and criteria. Determine if your organization and its needs are a match with the foundation's giving profile. If they are, proceed. If not, seek another need or another benefactor. Outline your need as a request that specifies fund needs and how the money will be used to provide services and products to benefit certain audiences. You can develop several draft levels of funding, as you do not want to be screened out by asking for too much or miss an opportunity by asking for too little. With this ammunition in your hunter's pack, you will be ready to approach a potential donor.

There are many foundations whose missions and purposes allow them to provide support to public libraries in need. These range from the very large such as the Bill and Melinda Gates Foundation, with hundreds of millions of dollars at its disposal, all the way down to small, local community foundations providing grants of $1,000. They all share one overriding characteristic: they were created to give support to worthy organizations and individuals. As stated earlier, the secret is to successfully match their need to give with your need to receive.

In selecting a grant opportunity to pursue, scheduling is important because most foundations and granting agencies operate on prescribed annual or even biennial grant cycles. If you miss a cycle, you might have to wait for the next round to begin.

There are a variety of online and print information resources available to help you identify potential sources of grants. You will get the most up-to-date information online. Using a web crawler such as Google or MetaCrawler, you can search under "library grants" and find quite a few sources of information listed. Here are a few grant-finding Internet websites that I have found useful:

Internet Library for Librarians (http://www.itcompany.com/inforetriever/ grant.htm). Contains a section titled "Library Grants" which provides links to grant-writing resources, search engines for grant resources, sites providing funding for projects, grant proposal guides and forms, and charitable foundations policy information. Its scope is far broader than library science.

Library Grants Blog (http://librarygrants.blogspot.com). Up-to-date listing of current library grant solicitations from a variety of organizations.

Grants for Libraries Hotline (www.quinlan.com). A print and online subscription service ($187 per year) offering weekly updates on grant opportunities and instruction on grant writing.

University of Wisconsin–Madison, Grants Information Center (http://grants .library.wisc.edu). Provides a good guide titled "Resources for Nonprofit Organizations."

GrantSmart (www.grantsmart.org). A comprehensive site which uses IRS tax return reports to compile a database currently containing 625,350 tax returns filed by 104,060 private foundations.

Technology Grant News and Grant Index (www.technologygrantnews.com). A subscription-service ($35 per year) index to grants for libraries and museums.

Grantsmanship Center, Funding Sources Guide (http://tgci.com/funding .shtml). Includes top grant-making foundations by state, corporate giving programs by state, community foundations by state, and state government home pages.

In print format, you can consult the references cited in the bibliography and the *Chronicle of Philanthropy*'s Guide to Grants (http://www.philanthropy.com/grants/), a database containing all foundation, corporate, and nonprofit grants listed in the *Chronicle of Philanthropy* since 1995. For an annual subscription price of forty-nine dollars, subscribers have complete access to the entire database, with search capabilities by grant maker, recipient, or subject. The database is updated every two weeks.

When seeking to identify foundations that might provide a grant to your library, I suggest you start at the local level. This offers the greatest chance of success and the least amount of competition, although local levels of grant funding are not as great as those of the large national foundations. In addition, local foundations usually have simpler application procedures and quicker award cycles than the major philanthropic organizations. You can identify potential local benefactors by searching the databases cited above, scanning local newspapers for notices of grant opportunities, or simply looking under the heading "Foundations-Educational, Philanthropic, Research" in your local Yellow Pages directory. Contact the foundations and ask about their grant eligibility criteria, amount limits, and schedules. It would probably be wise to mention whether your public library is classified as an IRS 501(c)(3) educational and charitable institution.

For several years, my library has received modest grants from local foundations, ranging from $1,500 to $10,000. Some of these grants required written applications stating a discrete need (e.g., library shelving, a children's computer, courses for seniors, etc.), while other, smaller grants were available merely for the asking with no written application being necessary. Some grants we received were unsolicited and were provided because our library publicity had made the foundations aware of our good works and needs.

Government Grants

A variety of federal government agencies provide both competitive and noncompetitive grant opportunities for independent public libraries. Among these are the Institute of Museum and Library Services (IMLS; see "LSTA Grants" below), National Science Foundation, National Endowment for the Humanities, National Endowment for the Arts, National Institutes of Health, and so on. The best source for global information on federal grant opportunities is the daily *Federal Register* published both in print and online (http://www.gpoaccess.gov/fr/index.html) by the Office of the Federal Register, National Archives and Records Administration, and available through the Government Printing Office. State government grant opportunities are usually listed on a state's official website and are usually also advertised by state libraries.

Soliciting grants from a governmental agency is typically a more formal and defined process than dealing with private foundations or individuals. There is often a formal "request for proposal" (RFP) or "request for applications" document issued with specified grant submission instructions, schedule, eligibility criteria, project categories, and funding limits. A good place to start when investigating government grants available to libraries is your county library center or state library. Many district, county, and state libraries maintain an advisory office, which keeps track of state and federal grant opportunities available to local public libraries. Once you identify your county or state's public library advisor, let them know your grant-seeking interests and they can advise you accordingly. My library's state-funded district library consultant assists libraries in both identifying grant opportunities and preparing the applications. She also facilitates partnering among libraries on joint grant applications. Note that government agencies generally encourage joint grant applications. (See the discussion of partnering later in this chapter.)

LSTA GRANTS

Each year, under the provisions of the Library Services and Technology Act, millions of dollars in federal funds are provided for specific projects in U.S. public libraries of all sizes. These funds are available from the IMLS. The IMLS awards grant monies to state libraries that have filed approved five-year plans. Each state library then solicits applications for competitive grants from local public libraries and library systems within the state. Most grants are for single or multi-library annual projects for amounts of up to $50,000 in a typical LSTA grant cycle. The state issues a grant RFP solicitation in early summer, application proposals are due in September, and awards are made in February. Projects begin in the spring and are conducted within a one-year period. Quarterly narrative and financial reports and a final report are required from grant recipients.

LSTA grants are awarded in specific project categories that follow federal guidelines, which normally emphasize applying technology to improve public library services to specific clienteles. The 2007 LSTA categories were Assistive Technology, Digitization, Planning, Promotion and Public Awareness, Collection Development, Special Services Programs, and Training. Both single and multi-category library applications are accepted.

In pursuing an LSTA grant, you must work with your state library and district and/or county library or federated system. They usually work together to administer the grants and will provide grant applications and application guidelines. Many state libraries or county library systems also provide basic training on applying for LSTA (as well as other state and federal) grants. This instruction may take the form of a seminar, webinar, or published guidelines. If you are serious in pursuing a grant, do take advantage of any instruction offered and pay close attention. Government agencies are usually quite open in giving guidance on what will help you to put together a successful grant application.

CONSTRUCTION GRANTS

If your library is considering construction of a new facility or the expansion or improvement of an existing building, you might look into the availability of government and private grants to assist you in this effort. You can find out about these grant opportunities using the research resources cited above. Again, seek the advice and assistance of your state and county library agencies. Be advised, however, that obtaining government construction grants can be an extremely detailed, time-consuming, and bureaucratic process that can involve one to two years of planning, documentation, and fundraising. But the rewards can be a grant of hundreds of thousands (or perhaps a million or more) dollars. Construction grants will seldom cover the entire cost of a building's construction, however. The grant almost always requires that the requesting library raise a certain amount of matching funds.

For example, the Pennsylvania State Library offers substantial Keystone construction grants to public libraries. However, to be eligible for these funds, a public library must invest a year or more of effort in preparing an application, which must be submitted in partnership with the library's home municipal government. The application package must contain detailed construction plans prepared by architects and engineers, a detailed funding plan showing how matching funds will be obtained by the library, detailed schedules, and, of course, a clear statement of need. The construction grant package may also require that the applying library commit to adhering to certain wage and labor standards, such as observing prevailing wage guidelines in employing construction workers.

Unlike small project grants where the library director and staff can usually put the application together by themselves, construction grant applications may require the contribution of many players, both within and outside of the library's hierarchy. Normally, the library board will form a building committee, which includes trustees, staff, and members of the community. There is often also a building funding subcommittee formed to manage the generation of matching funds from the community and other sources. Try to include people on these committees who have construction and fund-raising experience. These committees may need to retain outside consultants and experts including architects, engineers, and fund-raisers if skilled volunteers cannot be found. If your state requires that your home municipality be a formal partner in the process (as in Pennsylvania), then a formal liaison and commitment with your town's engineering and budget officers will also have to be established. The committee should also designate its official liaison point with the state and other granting agencies, who will be responsible for coordinating the application preparation and submission process.

As with most government grants, state construction grant processes are usually competitive and have specific annual schedules for grant preparation and submission that must be adhered to. Again, take advantage of any instruction offered by the construction-granting agency, including seminars, websites, and publications. Establishing personal contact with grant agency officials is also useful and will help in resolving any specific questions which may arise. Do not be shy about asking grant agency officials for advice on how to make your submission more acceptable to them. You may be surprised at how much they may tell you, because by ensuring that your library's submission is complete and correct, they are making their job of evaluation easier.

Partnering

Grant agencies like proposals in which the primary grant requester enhances the probability of project success and benefits by citing a partner or two as part of the proposed team. You can basically select between two types of partners: (1) a co-beneficiary, such as another public library, that will share the grant funding, grant effort, and grant benefits with you, or (2) a strategic partner that provides needed project skill expertise that is not available at your library. Strategic partners come in all flavors. They can be institutions or individuals, not-for-profits or businesses, local or distant. Their participation should be in accordance with a clearly defined role and should yield expected benefits such as improved results, cost savings, or reduced duplication of effort. If your partner will provide its contribution to the project on a pro bono basis, this should be made clear, because it really strengthens your proposal.

My library's recent LSTA grant to improve services to seniors and the home-bound serves as an example. The granting agency required that the project include a survey and statistical evaluation task to validate its effectiveness in achieving its stated goals. We did not possess the skills to perform such a task in our library, but we were able to enlist a research institute at a local university. The institute's director himself contributed to the proposal, designed the survey instruments, and analyzed the survey results, all on a pro bono basis. The granting agency was delighted. If you do intend to partner on your grant, get a letter of commitment from your partner and include it in the grant application package that you submit.

Writing Your Grant

Once you have targeted a grant-funding agency, confirmed your library's eligibility and needs against the agency's criteria, and decided on what you are going to ask for (including how much and why), you can begin the process of writing the grant proposal.

A grant proposal is a fairly stylized piece of marketing literature which may be characterized as a cross between a technical report and a sales brochure. The grant-seeking institution is selling its credentials, its project's value, and its need to the evaluating reader(s) who have funds to give away to support good works. If the grant process is competitive, your grant proposal must also convince the evaluators that your institution and proposed project are more worthy of the grant than those of other competing institutions. Your grant proposal is often all the review panel will employ to make their award decisions, so it must tell your whole story in a clear, concise, and convincing manner.

How does one learn to write a winning grant proposal? There are several alternatives. You can read a manual on the subject, such as Stephanie Gerding and Pam MacKellar's book *Grants for Libraries: A How-to-Do-It Manual.* Or you can consult the various websites and subscription newsletters that I cited earlier in this chapter. You can take a course on grant writing if one is offered by your county or state library support agency, or sign up for a commercial grant-writing seminar such as the Grantsmanship Training Program offered by the Grantsmanship Center (http://tgci.com/gtptraining.shtml) for an $825 tuition fee. If you have the time, money, and inclination to pursue these avenues then by all means do so, although few small public library staff or trustees may be able to afford such luxuries. I believe you can also be successful in the grant pursuit process through the application of disciplined on-the-job training. If you have never "written a grant," it is normal to feel a bit intimidated at first, but like learning how to swim, the best way is to jump right in.

No one can guarantee that your grant proposal will win, but here are some basic rules for proposal writing that will help to ensure a responsive, relevant proposal that will be taken seriously by the grant evaluators. These guidelines are drawn from my decade of experience as a professional proposal writer in industry and, more recently, five years of writing grants in a small public library.

Study and Analyze the Grant Solicitation

Invest time in studying the granting agency's grant solicitation documents, criteria for awards, and statement of mission and goals, particularly those that pertain to the agency's grant activities. In grant writing, treat the request for proposal as your bible and ten commandments and follow its instructions religiously. Highlight what appear to be the principal foci of the organization as stated in its documentation. Underline what seem to be buzzwords and phrases that are important to the organization. Determine which action verbs are used with frequency in the documents.

What you are doing here is establishing what the focus of the organization's grant giving is and what hot buttons you should cite in your application to demonstrate your mutual commitment to the same ideals. Put aside your pride of authorship and write your proposal using the words and style from the granting agency's literature. Your grant proposal's vocabulary will then be comfortably familiar and understandable to the grant evaluators because you are using their language. In the grantsmanship game, familiarity between grantor and grantee, rather than breeding contempt, facilitates award. Granting agencies make awards to organizations that demonstrate similar understanding and values.

If the grant solicitation document provides suggested headings for sections of the proposal, be sure to use them in your response, verbatim. Employ the RFP's headings and structure if you can. It is likely that the folks who evaluate your grant proposal are the same ones who wrote the grant solicitation document. They may not appreciate your rewriting their words, but conversely will take your acceptance of their language as a positive sign of cooperativeness. Simply stated, the more closely you follow the rules in preparing and submitting your grant request, the higher your probability of success.

Follow All the Rules

Study the grant solicitation's rules and conditions and follow them to the letter. Use the RFP's headings and structure in your proposal. What I like to do is to cut and paste the grant agency's RFP headings as the outline for my proposal to ensure that I am compliant in my writings. Stick to the RFP-specified format, structure, and word count. Comply with the RFP submission schedule and delivery requirements religiously. If the RFP specifies that proposals must be received by 5:00 p.m. on a certain date, submitting it at 5:05 will likely mean that it will not be considered. With more and more agencies going to electronic submission of grants, it is important to get confirmation that your grant application was electronically delivered on time. Therefore, it is appropriate to ask that the grant receiver confirm the receipt of your e-proposal by return e-mail.

Don't omit anything that is called for in the solicitation. Even if a requested information element is not relevant to your organization, respond in the appropriate section by stating "not applicable" or something similar. Demonstrated responsiveness and the ability of the potential grantee to follow instructions is an important, albeit unstated, criterion for most granting institutions.

If you are unsure how to respond to a particular RFP requirement, contact the granting agency to ask for clarification. I have found that asking valid questions during the proposal-writing phase may actually help in building rapport. However, a word of caution here: it is OK to ask questions about proposal submission procedures or formats, but do not ask about "technical" matters on which you should be knowledgeable, such as the running of a public library and responding to its patrons. Asking a naive question can hurt you by creating questions in an evaluator's mind about your understanding and ability to successfully conduct the project.

Discretionary Proposal Outline

Occasionally, you may be called upon to write a grant proposal for which there is no prespecified format. Therefore, you will have to ensure that your proposal clearly states the Why, What, and How of your proposed project. If put in this position, you might want to consider the following proposal format that I have evolved and successfully employed both as a public library "grantsman" and in my prior life as a "Beltway bandit" government contractor.

1. Overview and Executive Summary (write this last)
2. Statement of Need (the problem to be solved by the grant; the Why)
3. Technical Proposal (project details and the solution to the problem; the What)
4. Management Proposal (schedule, staffing, resources; the How)
5. Evaluation of Results (proof the grant money was well spent)
6. Cost Proposal (how much you want plus any cost sharing)
7. Qualifications Statement (why they should award the grant to you)
8. Promotion Plan (good PR for grantor and grantee)
9. Appendixes

Each of these sections of the proposal is treated in detail below.

OVERVIEW AND EXECUTIVE SUMMARY

The proposal's overview and executive summary is a concise abstract or thumbnail of the entire proposed project. Write it last, after all other sections have been completed, to ensure it is accurate and comprehensive. When I was a government contractor writing proposals for a living, my boss advised me to take particular care in writing the executive summary, the management proposal, and the cost proposal sections because his twenty years of experience convinced him that proposal evaluators in a hurry look only at these parts.

STATEMENT OF NEED

The proposal's statement of need should clearly state the Why of the proposed grant. State the problem or problems the grant will address and solve. To the extent possible, relate the need addressed by the proposed project to the granting agency's mission and purpose. It helps to cite statistics such as the number of library patrons and specific segments of the community who will benefit from the proposed project. Highlight any groups that may be the focus of the granting agency, such as seniors, minorities, handicapped, preschoolers, and so on. "Outcome-based results" is a popular concept among granting agencies, so stating needs in terms of expected results can be effective in this section as well as in the evaluation of results section below.

TECHNICAL PROPOSAL

The technical proposal section presents the What of the proposed grant project. Here is where you summarize each of the project's specific tasks, their sequence, interrelationships, and expected results. Empathize with the reader here. It is important to employ the appropriate level of technical jargon and detail required by the anticipated evaluator. If the proposal is to your state library, such as a request for an LSTA grant, the evaluator will be a librarian, so a fairly deep level of library science-related detail and jargon is not only acceptable but expected. However, if your grant request is to a community philanthropic foundation, then arcane library jargon should be eschewed and an explanation of basic public library operation should be given.

MANAGEMENT PROPOSAL

The management proposal should provide an explanation of "How" resources and time will be managed on the proposed project to achieve desired results. Among elements to be discussed here are scheduling, staffing, partnering, reporting, and allocation of other nonstaff resources. State how internal library management systems and policies will be employed to ensure effective project management, quality control, and achievement of expected results. The makeup of the proposed project team and its leadership should also be clearly stated here, with cross-reference to their biographies in an appendix. Clearly state whom you intend to partner with and the partner's specific role and skills. If you have a letter of commitment from the partner, reference it here and include it in an appendix.

EVALUATION OF RESULTS

You should also include in your proposal a section on how you will evaluate project results versus project objectives, in order to help inspire confidence among the evaluators. This will assure the granting agency that the positive impact of its grant to you will be objectively measured and reported.

COST PROPOSAL

The cost proposal presents the total project itemized budget, including how much money is being requested, how much matching funds will be provided by the library and its partners, and how the funding will be allocated among the proposed project's tasks. Present a complete project budget with cost projections matched to the project tasks and schedule, and itemized by expenditure category such as labor, purchased materials, travel, outside consultants, and so on. Clearly differentiate between funds from the grant and matching funds from the library and its partners. Unless prohibited, in most cases you can also consider the market value of noncash services and goods as matching funds. By doing this, the library can increase the amount of its matching funds by dollarizing the values of its in-kind contributions to the project such as labor, facilities, expendable materials, travel, and overhead. Even the estimated value of volunteer labor can be considered as a matching contribution. This is important, since the amount of outside grant funding is often proportional to the amount of matching internal funding.

QUALIFICATIONS STATEMENT

The qualifications statement is designed to tell the granting agency why it should award the grant to your library, and is also intended to inspire confidence in your ability to successfully conduct and conclude the proposed project. Therefore, put modesty aside here and brag about the personal qualifications and relevant experience of your project team. Be sure to showcase the qualifications of the project team leader (sometimes called the principal investigator) as they relate to the project. You should also cite any similar successful efforts that the library may have conducted. You should cross-refer project team resumes, letters of commendation, and awards in this section to the detailed documents in an appendix. Do not forget to also cite the qualifications of any partners who will contribute to the project such as consultants, educators, associations, or government officials and include their resumes, awards, and letters of commitment in an appendix.

PROMOTION PLAN

Supporting good works may be the primary objective of granting institutions, but virtually all of them appreciate some good publicity. Therefore, you should include a section on how you plan to publicize the proposed project and its results in your proposal. Cite how you will use effective PR techniques to make the media and public aware of the grant project. It is good protocol to offer to have the granting agency review any press releases or other pieces of literature that cite its name.

APPENDIXES

Use appendixes to the grant application proposal to include any supplemental information that will help present your case. This can include resumes of the principal investigator and key personnel, library organization charts, letters of commitment from partners, sample forms or survey questionnaires, statistical tables, examples of the library's prior relevant experience, awards and honors, and the like. For example, in an LSTA grant proposal to the state requesting funds for a project to aid seniors, we included newspaper clippings citing our prior activities for this target group in the appendixes.

Proposal Writing Style

Some might say that proposal writing embodies a distinct literary style. I believe there is some truth in this. I have found that a proposal's narrative comes across better if written as short, precise statements in a positive mode using action verbs in the first-person plural, future tense.

As examples, use statements such as "In month one we [or the XYZ Library] will perform the following tasks: . . . ," "Phase one shall be the implementation of . . . ," or "In this task we will define [or investigate, or create, or evaluate, etc.] . . ." Remember, faint heart never won fair grant. Write with confidence, as if you are certain the proposed project will be successful. Avoid "iffy" phrases such as "we hope," "hopefully," "with luck," "maybe," or "if possible." If your proposal exudes uncertainty or lack of confidence, it is unlikely that it will be a winner.

When you write, concentrate on producing simple, clear sentences. Do not obfuscate. Be precise. Do not be subtle about important points such as the need for the project and its anticipated benefits. If appropriate, cite potential harm to the community by not undertaking the project.

Grant agencies want to be reasonably sure they are investing in successful projects that will yield productive results, not in potential failures. This does not mean that you must guarantee in advance that each and every project you propose will be 100 percent successful. If there is an element of risk involved in your proposed project (and there almost always is some), identify it and directly address the steps you will take to minimize the chance of failure and maximize the probability of success. For example, if you are requesting funding for a teen reading program, you can recognize up front that it is difficult to attract youth to the library in today's world. In your proposal you can then cite this risk and how you will minimize it by proposing fallback measures such as outreach to youth groups; partnerships with school reading counselors, and so on.

If submitting your proposal in online or another electronic format, certain precautions can save you time and ensure your proposal's acceptability. Most e-proposals impose limits on the maximum number of typed characters or words permitted in each section. In addition, most e-proposal templates do not include spelling or grammar checkers. You can both ensure compliance with word limits and avoid typographical errors in your proposal via the simple expedient of writing each proposal section first as a Microsoft Word page, running it through the spell and grammar checker, and doing a word or character count (found under the "Tools" heading on the toolbar) before copying it and dropping it into your e-proposal. The Word pages can also be saved as backup copies of your proposal.

As a final step, ask someone unfamiliar with the proposed project to review what you have written to determine if it is clear and makes sense. Then have someone familiar with the RFP and your library's needs review your application to see if you have covered all the points or if anything has been omitted. Moreover, check to see whether your board or any other library officials need to review any of these documents. Make your final editorial changes, put together the application package, deliver it to the grant agency, and then sit back and await the notice of grant award. Congratulations, you are now a member of the "grantsman" fraternity.

CHAPTER EIGHT

ONGOING MARKETING OF YOUR LIBRARY AND ITS PROGRAMS

One might ask why a public library would concern itself with marketing. The answer to this conundrum is simple. The small public library must master and employ the tools of modern marketing to attract and influence current and potential patrons as well as current and potential benefactors. It needs to use marketing to encourage use of its facilities and services and to ensure adequate and continuing support. A public library has to keep its constituents and its supporters continually aware of its activities and value to the community. It does so via the tools of marketing.

In this chapter we will look into some marketing techniques that are applicable to public libraries. The bibliography gives references for further study, and you might also want to look at the following library marketing websites:

Library Support Staff.com, Marketing Our Libraries, http://www.library supportstaff.com/marketinglibs.html

Chris Olson and Associates, Marketing Treasures: The Electronic Newsletter with Marketing Ideas for Information Professionals, http://www.chrisolson.com/marketingtreasures/mtresources.html

American Library Association, Toolkit for Winning Support for Your Rural Library, http://www.ala.org/rural/advocacytoolkit.htm

In a broad sense, marketing has five basic components:

1. Defining target populations and their needs
2. Creating an awareness of your organization and its offerings
3. Promoting specific products and services
4. Closing the sale and delivering the product
5. Evaluating customer satisfaction

Let us look at how these may be applied to a small public library's environment.

Tailoring Your Marketing to Your Target Audiences

Chapter 2 introduced the concept of market segmentation as a means of linking library services to each part of your community. This approach applies equally well in the "marketing" of your library and its services to these same community segments. As we discussed earlier, there are three broad target communities to be addressed by the public library: (1) current library patrons, (2) potential library patrons, and (3) funding and support groups.

Just as you need to develop specific library services to meet the needs of different library user communities, you have to also consider developing specific marketing approaches for your various user and supporter communities. This includes both how you represent the library as an institution and how you keep your community up-to-date on library happenings. It does not mean that you develop separate approaches for each community you serve. Indeed, these groups are not mutually exclusive, since you may find that your greatest donors are among your regular users and volunteers. It therefore may be best to develop a baseline public relations approach and slant it, as appropriate, to suit the perspectives of the various audience segments you serve. However, you may have to be more selective with the media channels and tools you use for various audiences. For example, you would probably employ a different approach for promoting a teen event than you might use for a seniors program.

Establishing a Consistent Library Image and Message

Think about the library's message that you want to get across to each group you serve and the best means of delivering it. This is what marketing people term "branding." What image does the library want to create in the minds of its intended audiences? How do you want the public to perceive your library as an institution? You might even want to consider the library as an institutional personality.

Suggested image concepts include the following:

the community's lifelong learning center

the university of the people

a "third place," or safe community refuge

a friendly gathering place for sharing knowledge

a one-stop information supermarket

a gateway to new information technologies

a "fun" place

a place to answer your questions

an extension of the school

a community center and a destination

an information and educational resource

a source of free knowledge and recreation

a business information headquarters

the learning place for those not served by any other information institution

You can present slightly different (but compatible) images, or library facets, to different user groups. For example, you might represent the library to teens as a "fun" knowledge-sharing refuge; to parents as an aid to accelerated learning; and to seniors as a continuing education center. This is merely good niche marketing and is why General Motors sells Corvette sports cars, Sierra pickup trucks, and Cadillac limousines.

Once you focus on the library image (or images) you want to put forth, be consistent in its representation and try to reflect the image via a "house style" in your promotional materials, which should include a characteristic, easily recognizable logo and a distinctive publication format. Some libraries may prefer a conservative image, and some may want to be flamboyant. Select the personality that is most comfortable to both your library and the community. In our library we ensure market image consistency by designating a single senior staff member, who reports to the library director, as our community relations coordinator. We delegate to her oversight of the preparation and dissemination of all marketing materials and the maintenance of all public relations databases and websites.

Selecting the Right Promotional Media Tools to Get Your Message Across

You can employ the mass media both to create a general awareness of your organization and its offerings and to promote specific events and services. These media include newspapers, radio, and TV. We have found that there are four basic mechanisms for getting the word out through the news media:

- press releases
- feature articles or news spots
- library columns
- paid advertising

Each of these types is discussed below.

Press Releases

The press release can be a powerful publicity tool for the small public library. A program of regularly issued press releases on noteworthy library events can ensure continued positive media coverage. We find that local newspapers and TV stations are always looking for "filler" pieces to round out each issue or newscast. They appreciate well-written press releases, and although they may not print all of them, you might be surprised at how much exposure you can receive. Since our library initiated a program of regular releases to a tested media list, we are frequently cited in virtually every newspaper, magazine, and every TV and radio station in our region. A release on a major story, such as winning a national award, usually gets us front-page coverage in the papers.

DEVELOPING YOUR MEDIA LIST

The first step in a successful public relations program is developing a rapport with key media contacts. Do some research and develop a comprehensive classified media list. Whenever possible, have the addresses you record include the name of a responsible individual rather than just the name of the paper or station. Include in your list the news, community events, book page, and feature editors, columnists, and reporters (both regular and freelance) for the key newspapers and news desks, and the anchors of the TV and radio stations in your area. Be sure to include the "community bulletin board" editors of the cable and public TV and radio stations in your media list. Add the regional as well as local media to your list. For example, my library also sends press releases to the media in our state capital, and they will frequently cover our events. Do not omit regional travel, business, and religious periodicals, since they too are looking for good, wholesome news features.

Your media list does not have to be limited only to "media" organizations. Your library can also benefit by sending your releases to your supporters and others of influence. For example, we include major foundation directors, corporate CEOs, chamber of commerce heads, elected officials, and university leaders on our press release mailing list. Also be sure to send your releases to your county and state library officials, as they like to be kept aware of public library accomplishments.

The person responsible for issuing your press releases can save a lot of time and effort if she uses a mailing list program (e.g., Excel) to build and maintain your list and to generate your mailing labels. Be sure to employ software that is e-mail compatible, since many news organizations now prefer to receive their press notices online. There is no prescribed "correct" size for a mailing list, since it should reflect the scope and extent of the media in your area. My library's list contains about fifty names.

It helps to have your community relations coordinator establish a personal rapport with the editors and reporters whose beat covers your geographic area or the education and not-for-profit sectors. Visit with these folks, invite them to your library events, and ask them how they would like to receive your press releases (e.g., e-mail, U.S. mail, fax, etc.). Attaching a friendly face to the name on your releases can improve your press relations and will facilitate getting your pieces placed.

PRESS-RELEASE WRITING STYLE

In my corporate marketing experience, I have learned that a properly formatted and well-written press release that fits the style of the target news media has a high probability of being published. (Appendix G contains a suggested model press-release format and a sample release.)

The first rule in preparing a winning press release is to write it so that the paper or news commentator can use it with little or no modification. Minimal editing of your release by the media will also ensure that your message gets across accurately in the way you intended. Study the language found in the articles of the newspapers you are targeting, especially the articles with bylines from the reporters on your media list. It is advisable to write your release in the third person, as if a reporter was writing it. Instead of saying "We are planning to present a program on . . . ," say instead "The XYZ Library is planning to present a program on . . ."

Segment your press release into stand-alone paragraphs. The first paragraph should give an overview summary. Each succeeding paragraph should then give successively more detail, with the concluding paragraph providing information on who to contact for additional information. This press-release writing technique is known in the trade as building in "get-off points." This is done because newspapers often employ press releases as "fillers" to make up a full paper. The get-off points allow the paper to employ as much (or as little) of the press release as it needs to fill its empty spaces. If you provide the get-off points, then you can ensure the stories about your library make sense, even if only part of your release is used.

PRESS RELEASE CONTENT

Public relations experts generally acknowledge that the content of your release should address "the five Ws": who, what, when, where, and why.

In determining which "whos" and "whats" might be worthy of a press release, consider that virtually any noteworthy event can merit a press release. We issue releases very liberally to announce such things as library programs, new services, new hires, new board or Friends officer appointments, staff service anniversaries, winning of an award or grant, and receiving a major donation. My view is that when in doubt, send a release out, because it is impossible to guess what will pique the interest of a reporter. For example, a release about our library's Friends book sale made a passing mention of our beginning to sell collectible surplus books on eBay. A reporter got excited about this aspect and did an article featuring our online sales efforts.

If you are promoting an event, be sure the press release includes the when and where of time, date, and place, as well as instructions on how to sign up for the activity.

Be clear in describing the purpose of the event or the objective of the press release, the why. Do not be subtle here. If it is a benefit event that is being announced, be clear on the library's financial needs and how the proceeds will be employed to improve library service to the community. If it is an award or major donation that is being acknowledged, cite the criteria that made the library worthy of the honor and include a quote from the awarding agency if appropriate. News media love quotations from high-ranking officials.

Emphasize both the unusual and the human-interest elements that might catch the attention of the media. For example, an announcement for our library benefit auction included a list of unusual items to be put on the block such as a ride in the police chief's cruiser, lunch with the mayor, and a fire hydrant and a manhole cover. This strange stuff caught the attention of a daily newspaper's weekend section editor, who wrote a half-page feature article on our sale. The editor said she never does features on auctions, but the unusual items in our release made her change her mind. In another release, we cited a mother and daughter team on our staff as our longest-tenured employees. The editor of our town weekly liked the human-interest aspect of the story and put a photo of the two gals on the paper's front page under the heading "The Library's First Family."

Including a photo with the press release is optional. If you send press releases as e-mail attachments, it is relatively simple to also attach a digital photo. If sending paper copies, photos should be high quality on good photo-stock paper. Ask the editors and writers what they prefer. Some papers will gladly use your submitted courtesy photo, while others will prefer to send their own photographer if they need a shot.

It is useful to create a standard one- or two-paragraph background blurb on your library's history and scope that can be included in each press release. Any special awards or recognition won by the library can also be cited here.

DISSEMINATING YOUR PRESS RELEASES

Send your press releases out to your media list at least two weeks prior to the event being announced. You may have to do a two-phase mailing, sending one batch by e-mail and another by the U.S. mail. As cited earlier, a consistent media image is important, so it is good practice to design and use a distinctive press-release letterhead format with the necessary contact information for your library and with a catchy title (e.g., "XYZ Library News Beat"). A distinctive press-release envelope is an option.

Feature Articles or News Spots

Press releases can be powerful tools in earning your library recognition and support. If a provocative press release generates enough interest at a newspaper, magazine, or TV station, they may opt to do a feature byline article or news spot. When this happens, a reporter, newscaster, photographer, or camera crew may visit your library to interview and "shoot" involved staff, volunteers, and patrons. Alternatively, the interviews may be conducted remotely by telephone or even via e-mail dialogue, and they may ask you to supply the photos. Let the reporter call the play and do what is comfortable for him.

In one instance, one of my library's press releases prompted a TV news anchor person and her cameraman to pay us a visit and ride along with me in the library van as I made my delivery rounds to the homebound. As a result, our new homebound delivery service was highlighted in a three-minute TV spot on the local NBC affiliate's 6:00 p.m. news, featuring an interview with a 98-year-old homebound library patron. This favorable coverage generated a number of unsolicited cash donations toward the continuation of this service. It also yielded positive feedback from our state library, whose LSTA grant had funded the establishment of the featured service. The state even requested a video copy of the newscast to share with the U.S. congressional committee that oversees the national LSTA grant program. Grant-giving agencies just love publicity on the positive impact of their grants. Be sure to let them know when this happens.

You may also be able to get a feature article without a press release. This is where personal rapport with a news editor or reporter comes in handy. You can politely suggest to the newsperson that you have a "hot" story that might be of interest to the paper's readers, citing unique features of the happening. If they have the space available, likely as not they may come out and cover your event with an article, giving you some good publicity. It is important not to abuse your newsperson relationships, so reserve the personal approach for really special, not routine, events. You can cement your reporter relationships by sending them a thank-you note for a really nice piece on your library, with a copy to their editor or publisher.

Library Columns

Library columns are great for getting your institution regularly scheduled media exposure. There are basically two types of library-related news columns to consider: the narrative conversational story mode and the factual list mode. Both types offer valuable PR tools for the public library.

Nancy Pearl, the charming librarian at the Seattle Public Library, has built a second career by producing television programs, radio commentaries, book reviews, and books (see, for example, *Book Lust*, 2003) for the general public on the topics of books and libraries. You too, on a local level, can emulate Nancy by writing a library column for your hometown newspaper. Local weeklies are often strapped to find good space fillers and may be receptive to an offer to do a weekly, biweekly, or monthly library column. I discovered this when, by coincidence, a new weekly regional newspaper, the *Donegal Ledger*, started up at the same time I was hired as director of the Milanof-Schock Library. The new editor, fishing for articles to bulk out her new creation, invited me to do a weekly column (which by mutual agreement was later reduced to biweekly and then monthly as I began to run out of ideas and the editor began to fill more space). This column, which I publish under the name Bibliofile, has been running for nearly five years. It has, I believe, generated a lot of favorable publicity for our library.

If you decide to write a column, you can include many things in it. You can do book reviews as Nancy Pearl does or, as I do, write about what interests you. In time I demonstrated to my editor that I would not get the newspaper in trouble with my written ramblings, and I am now allowed considerable latitude in what I write about. I often do columns on the library and its collections (e.g., suggested theme readings and movies for Valentine's Day, Halloween, Memorial Day, etc.; the library book sale; National Library Week; the year's best books; interesting items at the forthcoming library auction; testimonials to outstanding library staff and volunteers, etc.). I balance pure library stuff with columns on local history and interesting places to visit, as well as local culture. Eating is one of the major pastimes of my geographic region, so I regularly do columns on the history of seasonally popular dishes such as chicken corn soup, shoo fly pie, or sauerkraut. I sometimes let my imagination run wild, and two of my more bizarre columns were written in Pennsylvania Dutch dialect and 1950s jive talk.

However, no matter what topic I write about, I end each column with a paragraph or two plugging my library. For a topical column, I segue by stating: "To learn more about this subject, you can borrow these books or consult these websites at the public library . . ." and follow this with a brief bibliography. The final paragraph in each of my columns gives a summary of forthcoming library events and the library's hours, address, phone numbers, and e-mail and website addresses. I sometimes use the column to put in a pitch for more volunteers, donations to our book sale and auction, and even (as a private citizen) for political support of library-related legislation or government funding issues. A byproduct of my journalistic endeavor is that it has made me a virtual member of the newspaper team and has allowed me to establish a close rapport with the newspaper's editorial staff. They now have a hard time saying no when I request feature article coverage of a library event.

Another type of column employed by some libraries and requiring less literary effort is a list of forthcoming library events, new acquisitions, and other factual items. My library also does this in the form of the Book Nook, a quarter-page block that appears on each week's op-ed page of the *Donegal Ledger*.

Paid Advertising

Paid advertising has not been very popular among public libraries, perhaps because of its expense and because libraries can usually get free news coverage of their events. Paid space advertising does have its place under certain circumstances, though. One drawback of relying on pro bono news coverage of your library's activities via the press release is that you have no control over if, when, where, and how your news will appear in the newspaper. Furthermore, even library columns get changed by editors, and there are certain things you might want published that are not appropriate in a library column. Therefore, if you need to control exactly what will be stated, the date it will appear, where in the paper it will appear, and in what format and size, then you need to put the information in a paid advertisement.

My library uses paid ads for auction announcements listing items to be sold and for acknowledging donors because we want these messages to appear in a timely manner exactly as written and in a prominent location. If you do run a paid ad, ask if the newspaper has a not-for-profit rate and if you can do your own layout and provide camera-ready copy to conserve funds. Some public libraries have overcome the relatively high cost of advertising by seeking business sponsorship of ads and billboards promoting the library and its services.

Community-Focused Promotional Tools

There are a number of other communication tools that you can employ to focus the attention of your community on the library and its activities. These include community bulletin boards; library websites; newsletters; posters, signs, and banners; participation in meetings; and direct mail.

COMMUNITY BULLETIN BOARDS

You can keep your community aware of your library's offerings by placing your program schedules and event posters on your region's community bulletin boards, both conventional and electronic.

With permission, post your list of programs and your notices on all of the public bulletin boards in your area that you know of. This includes supermarkets, community centers, churches, schools, town halls, banks, realtors, courthouses, clubhouses, chambers of commerce, and the like. Establish one or more bulletin board routes and assign these to volunteers or staff who can hit the various sites on their way to and from the library.

Cable TV and radio stations, newspapers, and webcasters on the Internet often maintain print and virtual community bulletin boards listing or announcing forthcoming events at no charge for not-for-profit organizations. Be sure to send them your lists of library activities to allow them to announce your happenings.

WEBSITES

In this day of widespread Internet communication, it is incumbent on every public library to develop and maintain a well-designed website as a communication and marketing vehicle.

Designate a competent and reliable staff member or volunteer as your library's webmaster. This person will be responsible for building your website and keeping it up-to-date. If no one in your library is knowledgeable in web page design, try to enlist one of the independent website designers in your area to provide the expertise on a pro bono basis in return for favorable mention in the library's website and newsletter.

Study other websites and Internet design manuals to come up with an attractive, uncluttered layout for your home page. Be sure to include hyperlinks to related websites such as your OPAC, the county library, and your municipalities, and ask them to reciprocate. You may also want to create temporary ancillary sites and links to pages for important events such as auction sales item lists, book sale details, book discussion groups, and so on.

We have found it quite valuable to also provide an e-mail link on the library website which we call Ask a Librarian. Via this link, we regularly receive e-mails asking reference questions, inquiring about programs, asking for directions, suggesting new titles for acquisition, offering to volunteer, or just saying thank you.

A major portion of your library's website can be dedicated to advertising library events and services (with or without links to registration forms), inviting people to become members, or soliciting donations. If you can, include some nice photos of the library, its staff, and volunteers. A library organization chart is optional. Always include in the website the library's address, phone and fax numbers, and hours of operation. If you have the space, also include directions to the library. Finally, do not let your website go stale. Update it at least weekly to encourage people to visit it often. Include a counter so you can tell how often your site is visited.

NEWSLETTERS

A library newsletter is a valuable communication vehicle that covers many bases. Whether it appears monthly or quarterly, use it to announce events, thank donors and volunteers, solicit donations, cite new acquisitions, introduce new staff, present an annual report, provide book reviews, or just about anything else.

Your newsletter does not have to be fancy and can be as simple as four or five pages produced on the library copy machine and stapled together. Develop a consistent format, a catchy title (e.g., "Library Ledger," "Biblio Beats," etc.), and appoint an editor from your staff, Friends, or volunteers. Establish (and make sure the editor enforces) a production schedule and you are off. To spread the load, you can assign topical newsletter columns to key volunteers and staff such as your board president, Friends president, library director, children's librarian, and so on.

We produce about 500 copies of our quarterly newsletter, which we then make available in the library and at key distribution points around the community (see "Bulletin Boards" above). You can also mail your newsletters out en masse or selectively to your various mailing lists.

POSTERS, SIGNS, AND BANNERS

You can use posters and signs of various sizes to announce library events, advertise library services, or solicit support. We produce these for display both inside the library and outside of it. We use posters in three sizes: letter (8.5" × 11"), poster (11" × 17"), and banners up to 15 feet long.

For internal library display, we typically use letter- and poster-size signs, which we produce on our computer printers and copiers. We post these on library bulletin boards as well as other strategic locations such as the children's area, over the water fountain, at the circulation desk, and even in the restrooms. For major events, such as our auction and book sale, we produce both small and large posters for display on community bulletin boards around the county.

I picked up on an interesting use for posters at a session on fund-raising at a recent Public Library Association conference. You can subtly gain library support from your community's political leaders by featuring them on READ posters. The ALA sells the Adobe Photoshop Elements software package for $129, which allows you to digitally insert a photograph of a local luminary holding a favorite book into a READ poster similar to the ones the ALA sells showing celebrities with their choice book. We bought the software, and now whenever a public official visits our library, we ask him to sit for these poster photos. We insert the honoree's photo into the READ poster by computer, along with a caption identifying the person and putting in a plug for the library and literacy. We print two copies of each poster, one for the library and one for the official's office. How can a public official then deny you support when on his office wall hangs a poster with his picture promoting public libraries and literacy?

For display around the county, we also produce small and large posters and banners. The posters are put up on community bulletin boards as discussed above. We usually do this only for major events, such as our benefit auction, that draw people from a wider area. To proclaim our annual book sale and auction, we string a fifteen-foot-long, three-foot-wide canvas banner across the main street business area two weeks prior to the sale. A sign painter and an arborist with a cherry picker crane assist us in this effort. Before you hang any banners from telephone poles across a public thoroughfare, however, first determine what permissions might be required from the local police, municipalities, and utility companies.

WORKING THE MEETINGS CIRCUIT

As mentioned previously, attending meetings of community and public service organizations is a good way to work up support for your library, get your message across, and make valuable contacts. Consider groups sharing common interests with the library such as education and literacy groups, community foundations, chambers of commerce, professional societies, veterans groups, fraternal orders, and service clubs such as the Lions, Kiwanis, Elks, Masons, Jaycees, Moose, and Rotary.

You can interface with these groups either as a meeting speaker or as an attendee. Many associations and clubs that meet regularly are always on the lookout for interesting speakers, and they will jump at the opportunity to let you speak about the library.

Over the past two years, I have been an invited speaker on the library at the meetings of such groups as the Business and Professional Women's Association, Lions, Kiwanis, chamber of commerce, and Society of Farmwives. If your library develops a standard presentation on its history, scope, services, and needs, then this task becomes relatively easy for a staff member or trustee to perform. Present a simple message on the library's community role, its history, services, and needs. Provide a concluding summary with a call for the reaction you desire from the group. If you use the canned package, put an appropriate spin on it to suit the interests of the particular group you are addressing. It can be useful to place your library presentation on the computer using Microsoft PowerPoint or equivalent so it is presentable and portable via a laptop computer and digital projector. Overhead projector transparencies are another low-cost alternative medium. When I speak about the library at one of the service clubs, I often go home with a donation check in my pocket because the raison d'être of most service clubs is to raise money to donate to needy community organizations, including the public library.

Attendance by staff and trustees at association meetings (membership optional) can also yield beneficial results for the library. By positively interacting with other meeting attendees (or "working the floor," as they say in industry), you not only impart information about the library, but also learn about community needs and make valuable contacts that can benefit the library in the future. For example, I represent the library in both the local chamber of commerce and the Lions Club. In fact, in 2006, to my surprise, I was nominated and elected to the office of president of the Mount Joy Lions Club. Beyond the personal satisfaction I derive from this, my contacts with these associations have yielded other benefits to the library, including joint events, volunteers, speakers, cash and equipment donations, and the opportunity to personally interact with a cross-section of community leaders whom I do not normally encounter at the library. I also believe that when library officials are prominent in community activities, they enhance their institution's visibility and stature.

DIRECT MAIL ADVERTISING

Direct mail is an important way of soliciting funds for public libraries, but is rarely used as a marketing tool. I think this lack of popularity stems from both its expense (even bulk mail costs about twenty cents per piece) and the reluctance among libraries to add their library's name to the "junk mail" deluge. Limited effectiveness may also be a factor.

We tried direct mail advertising and it did not pay off. Following the lead of another public library and the commercial auction houses, we decided to promote our benefit auction via direct mail in 2005. We sent out over 8,000 postcards to our library patron mailing list at a cost of about $1,500. We found that the mailing appeared to have no impact on auction attendance. The other public library I borrowed the idea from also came to the same conclusion, and we both shelved direct mail as a marketing technique for benefit auctions.

Direct mail library promotion, however, can be very effective on an individual patron basis. For example, consider reaching out to new arrivals in your community with invitations to visit the library and sign up for a card. Use newspaper birth announcements to invite new parents to come and check out your infant lap-sit programs. This personal approach really works!

The marketing industry considers direct mail as an effective promotion and sales technique, as evidenced by the volume of advertising materials most of us find in our mailboxes. If used judiciously, this technique might just work for your library as a promotional tool.

Closing the Sale and Follow-Up Marketing

In my prior life, I spent some time as a field salesperson and later became a field sales staff trainer. I taught that when the prospect says "I'll take it" and forks over his moola, the sale is "closed." In a library environment we "sell" our services, facilities, events, and collections to our patrons. Therefore, we might consider the sale as "closed" when a patron receives an answer to a reference question, borrows a book, employs a public online workstation, attends a library event, or uses a library study carrel.

However, in conventional sales, we also teach that follow-up after the sale is necessary to keep the sale closed and prevent "buyer's remorse," where the buyer changes his mind and asks for a refund. There is a related concern in the public library. Marketing and image maintenance must continue even after a patron visits the library and borrows a book. The library must continue to sell itself and its services before, during, and after each transaction. A grouchy circulation assistant or reference librarian can instantly negate all of the positive marketing effort and money spent to encourage people to use the library. Therefore, I recommend that all library job descriptions (including those for volunteers) clearly state that courtesy and a positive and pleasant demeanor are required. Furthermore, library staff should be trained on how to become knowledgeable of and how to advise patrons on all library services and events. This is really follow-up and continuous marketing. A rule in marketing is that the customer will judge you only by his or her last contact with you. To avoid losing patrons and patron goodwill, train your staff and configure your facilities to ensure that all interactions between library and patron are positive and will yield pleasant memories. Let every staff member and volunteer know that they each serve as a public library goodwill ambassador.

Another aspect of continuous marketing is keeping your public up-to-date on the library and its offerings, or what you might call "reinforcing the image." For example, at the beginning or end of a library program, why not give a little "commercial" for the library, perhaps citing its role as a lifelong learning center and its need for community support, and mentioning other library activities that might be of interest. Do not be afraid to take advantage of a captive audience when you have one, because your cause is a noble one.

Evaluating Customer Satisfaction

Ensuring customer satisfaction is critical if you want "repeat sales." Obviously, people may not return to your library if they are unhappy with the services they receive. Therefore, it is incumbent on the library to maintain an awareness of its patrons' satisfaction levels. There are a number of ways to ascertain patron satisfaction with your services. You can use a variation of the techniques cited in chapter 2 such as surveys and interviews. We place a suggestion box in our lobby with simple evaluation forms (name optional) and a sign asking patrons, "How Are We Doin'?" People drop their comments (both good and bad) in the box and we act on them. If a staff member gets a personal commendation placed in the box, then we publicly honor them with "atta-girl" or "attaboy" recognition gifts at our monthly library staff meeting.

I know of libraries that periodically distribute evaluation "report cards" for their patrons to fill out, and others that hold town meeting–type discussions with patrons to determine satisfaction levels. Whatever technique you employ, the important thing is to keep aware of how your patrons are reacting to your library and its offerings. You need to do this to ensure relevance and responsiveness to your community.

Now that you have some ideas on promoting your library and its activities, let us get down to looking at how we can create some really good programs that are worthy of advertising.

CHAPTER NINE

INNOVATIVE LIBRARY PROGRAMMING
ON A SHOESTRING

It is relatively easy to develop and present high-quality programs in your library if money is not a limiting factor. The real challenge is to formulate award-winning programs when you have little or no program development funds at your disposal. This chapter will give you some pointers on how to do this.

Responding to Your Audience's Interests

The principle that underlies all successful library programming, whether it costs a fortune or a farthing, is that it must appeal to the interests of the target audience. As stated previously, the library must be responsive to its constituency, and that goes double for topical event programming. Know your community and give them what they want. If you cannot accurately determine this in advance, you will learn by trial and error. This comes from someone who has planned what he considered to be great programs which virtually no one attended, contrasted with programs that I considered marginal but which drew standing-room-only crowds. Although timing, publicity, and even weather will affect attendance at a library event, a topic of high community interest will always bring them out.

For example, in my home Pennsylvania Dutch country where eating is one of the most popular pastimes, any library program on food will get good attendance. Once you have identified areas of potential interest to your patrons, you can imaginatively plan some programs around them that will not tax your library's budget, using some of the techniques below.

Seeking Presenters from the Whole Community

One way to present low-cost but interesting programs is to recruit pro bono expert presenters who will speak or do a demonstration at your library either because they are passionate about the topic, it is part of their job to make presentations, they hope to generate business, they possess a strong sense of community service, or they want to pay the library back for services they have received. Using this approach, we recruit volunteer speakers such as teachers as story readers

immigrants as ethnic cooking and culture teachers

bankers as investment and entrepreneurial instructors

university and high school faculty as computer tutors

MDs and nurses as health instructors

government employees talking about their programs (e.g., Social Security, Medicare, Environmental Protection Agency, etc.)

merchants introducing certain products and services in a nonsales mode

hobbyists and collectors

artists and craftsmen

conservationists

police and firefighters

travel agents

retirees talking about their trips

veterans sharing war experiences

Because the library provides a unique neutral venue, it can pull together a cross-section of speakers from disparate segments of the community as partners in interesting and informative programs. A good example was my library's Baby Boomer program series. In addressing the diverse interests and needs of the aging baby boomers, we put together a six-session program that included these presenters:

1. A county Office of the Aging speaker reviewing subsidized employment opportunities for seniors
2. A representative of Elder Hostel discussing low-cost educational tours
3. A computer teacher discussing the advantages offered by computers and the Internet
4. A geriatric psychiatrist on how to deal with the physical and mental effects of aging
5. A Social Security Administration official explaining Medicare and Social Security
6. An AAA travel agent presenting travel tips for seniors

This program series was a big hit, cost our library virtually nothing because all speakers were pro bono, and earned us the AARP Award of Excellence for Library Services for Older Adults in 2006 as well as some positive media coverage.

When you're putting together presentations or programs like this, check to see whether your library's bylaws, guidelines, or other rules require that speakers sign waivers or any similar releases. It might not always be necessary, but it can't hurt to check.

Holding Joint Programs

Another technique for mounting interesting and low-cost learning events is to hold joint programs in partnership with other organizations. Examples of groups we have done this with include the following:

American Association of University Women	investment clubs
business and trade groups	League of Women Voters
chambers of commerce	literary societies
chess clubs	martial arts clubs
community health services	military reenactors
culinary arts schools	model railroader clubs
dog-training schools	quilting groups
educator associations	service clubs
environmental and conservation groups	speakers bureaus
4H and Grange groups	sportsmen clubs
fraternal societies	toastmasters clubs
historical societies	wine-tasting groups

To facilitate regular joint programs, your library can even invite compatible not-for-profit clubs to meet in your library's community rooms. Our library has done this with a local investment club, a chess club, and a Moms Club.

Drawing Speakers from Within the Library

Do not overlook your library team as an internal speaker's bureau. Poll your staff and volunteers to determine what skills, training, vocations, avocations, and interesting trips they might be able to present as a library program. You might be surprised! We learned that the retired engineer who chaired the investment club also ran a hobby business farm raising alpacas. He agreed to bring a trailer load of the long-haired beasts to the library one summer Saturday, and we built a "Meet the Alpacas" event around the visit. Over 200 adults and children showed up! Other staff and volunteer skills we turned into programs included

- desktop publishing
- digital photography
- gourd decorating
- how to buy and sell on the Internet
- martial arts
- model railroad design
- quilting

- scrapbooking
- soup cooking
- travelogues on Africa and South America

In seeking a program to fill a gap in our schedule, we conceived a "hobby fair" and invited library staff and volunteers with interesting hobby collections to display them in our community room. The displays included Mickey Mouse mementos, snow globes, Beatles memorabilia, model airplanes, military miniatures, model trains, and giant Lego sculptures. The event was a big hit, and we plan to do it again.

Drawing Speakers from Among Your Patrons

You can invite library patrons with interesting backgrounds and skills to share them with others at the library. For example, we invite patrons who have emigrated to the United States from other parts of the globe to speak at our very successful Culture and Cooking series.

This series originated through a bit of serendipity. The library helped a newly arrived young geologist from Nairobi to get the information he needed to become certified as a high school science teacher. In keeping with his cultural traditions, he expressed the desire to "give back" something to the library. Instead of taking any of his limited cash, we suggested that he instead give a talk on his native land, Kenya, at the library. Aided by his ten-year-old son, he did so and as an added benefit prepared and shared samples of typical Kenyan dishes. The audience was thrilled, and a stolid Pennsylvania Dutch citizen was heard to remark with surprise, "Ach, these Kenyans are people just like us!"

With this favorable launch and its contribution to community understanding of ethnic diversity, we continue to suggest to new emigrants who visit our library that they might want to consider sharing their culture and cooking with their new community. The idea clicked, and over the last two years our Culture and Cooking series presentations have traversed the globe, highlighting such exotic places as

Bolivia	Germany	Norway
Costa Rica	Italy	Russia
El Salvador	Japan	South Africa
Ethiopia	Kenya	Thailand
France	Korea	Vietnam

We supplement each oral presentation with background handouts on the country being covered, including bibliographies, and we display library materials on the region that are available for loan. The library's only direct cost for these multicultural mini-festivals is to reimburse the presenters for food ingredients, and many graciously decline our reimbursement because they want to "give back" to the library.

CHAPTER TEN

STAFFING YOUR LIBRARY'S PLAN

Although I promised that this book would not address basic library operations, proper staffing is so critical to a small library's survival (and makes up such a large portion of its expenses) that I want to provide some guidance on how to optimize your staff resources despite limited funds. Perhaps one of the greatest challenges faced by the small public library is recruiting, training, and retaining high-quality staff with a limited budget. Here are some staffing techniques that can work for small public libraries.

Staff Recruiting and Scheduling

I link staff scheduling with recruiting because flexible scheduling has proven to be a very useful strategic recruiting tool. Although economic exigencies force our library to offer relatively low wages, we have still been able to attract qualified and dedicated workers because we offer very flexible part-time work hours.

Many people seem to find the offer of part- or flextime employment attractive because it allows them to better balance work with their other family, education, volunteer, and home business responsibilities. The downside of this flexible work approach is that it presents a challenge to the library administrators who schedule work hours. Although we encourage employees to work on set schedules, we tend to be very understanding about accommodating changes when employees request them in advance. Our library's assistant director maintains the work schedule, and all assignments and changes are cleared through her. However, very frequently, employees who need to change hours will make her task easier by trading work hours among themselves to ensure adequate coverage on each shift. We have evolved and perfected this system because for forty years the library employed only part-timers. In 2002 I became the library's first and only full-time employee.

An economic advantage (and alas, in our case, a necessity) of employing part-time staff is that they do not receive fringe benefits such as health insurance and pensions. I wish we could provide these benefits, but we cannot afford to, and most of our employees do not require them because they have medical coverage through their spouses or former employers. The few employees who have to buy health insurance can get discounts through our chamber of commerce's group plan.

As might be guessed, this mode of employment brings us a fair number of house-wives, retirees, and library school graduate students. These people offer a variety of interesting and useful education and experience plus a high degree of dedication. If our library ever reaches a point of economic stability where we can afford a full-time staff of M.S.L.S. degree holders, I doubt if their efficiency and dedication would be any greater than what we now achieve with our part-timers.

Tapping Community Sources of Volunteers

In an ideal world, public libraries would be able to meet their responsibilities by employing only paid staff without any need for volunteer labor. For most small public libraries, however, volunteer workers are necessary to get the job done. You can find the volunteers you need among a variety of sources in your community. Look first to your library's staff, board, and Friends. Many of these people have family members and friends who might be willing to assist on either an ad hoc or regular basis. Next, look to your library patrons. There are many regular library users who would be grati-fied to give back some volunteer effort to the library in return for the free library ser-vices they have received.

We solicit volunteers from the community in a variety of ways. We use word of mouth among patrons, staff, and volunteers; we post notices on library and community bulletin boards; we print our need in columns and in community newsletters; and we make announcements at club meetings. Consider working with interested groups such as teachers' unions and service clubs to get volunteers for major events.

A valuable group of pro bono help is what I call "conscripted volunteers." These are people who are required to perform community service for a number of reasons. They come in all ages, from kids to seniors. Young people include students required to perform community service internships by their schools or churches and scouts working on merit badges. If you are lucky, you might even be able to get a library school intern.

Check with your county Office of the Aging because it may have available federal funds to reimburse libraries that hire unemployed and needy seniors. Your county parole office may also have available some minor offenders who need to work off their infractions through community service. However, you will have to be selective regarding the latter two sources. When we employ community service "volunteers" from both the Office of the Aging and the parole office, experience forces us to impose certain preconditions, which the agencies readily accept. These include minimum standards for physical and mental dexterity, personal appearance, personality, literacy and English language ability, and the need to pass a child abuse clearance. From the probation office, we accept only first-time DUI offenders with no prior record. We have gotten some excellent, highly skilled volunteers in this mode, and many have continued as real volunteers after their mandatory service was completed, with several being hired later as paid employees.

Friends of the Library

An extremely valuable source of public library volunteer labor (especially with regard to fund-raising activities and programs) is a Friends of the Library group. Typically, this is a discrete group of volunteers created for the specific purpose of supporting the library by conducting fund-raising activities, organizing library programs, creating publications, and serving as a source of volunteer labor.

Throughout this book, I have cited numerous fund-raising activities which are conducted or supported by our Friends of the Library. Friends groups often have charters, elect officers, hold regular meetings, and may levy annual dues. In some libraries (such as mine) the Friends of the Library have established themselves as a separate 501(c)(3) not-for-profit corporation to ensure tax exemption and other benefits. I have included the bylaws of my library's Friends group in appendix H as a potential model for others interested in setting up a similar organization.

In setting up a Friends group, it might be useful to obtain the advice of the library's accountant or attorney and to determine if there is an umbrella organization for library Friends groups in your state. In Pennsylvania, for example, a group known as Pennsylvania Citizens for Better Libraries provides advice to library Friends associations and assists them in getting started.

Organizing Your Volunteers' Efforts

If a library makes regular use of volunteers, it may want to consider designating a library employee or volunteer as a "volunteer coordinator." This person can be made responsible for the recruiting, vetting, training, and scheduling of the volunteer team. This practice can increase the efficiency of your volunteer staffing and can preclude many of the problems some public libraries have experienced with inappropriate or improperly trained volunteers.

Staff Training

Proper staff training is very important if a library employs a significant number of staff and volunteers without prior library experience. Training can be facilitated by several low-overhead means, including

- development of understandable library procedure instructional manuals
- in-house training courses and on-the-job instruction by library supervisors
- monthly staff update meetings
- sending staff and volunteers to county and state library training classes and seminars

We employ all of these techniques in our library, and they seem to work well. In fact, our state library code requires that all paid clerical staff members receive at least three Continuing Education Unit (CEU) hours of relevant training annually, with professionals requiring eight CEU hours per year.

Choosing Trustees Wisely

The most important of a public library's volunteers are its board of trustees. Trustees, perhaps more than anyone else, hold the survival and future of the library in their hands, and therefore they should be selected very carefully.

The primary roles of a public library trustee are to plan for the future, to ensure fiscal viability, and to establish policy. In the small public library, board membership is not a ceremonial office but rather one that involves careful attention and effort. The old saw is that library board members should be selected on the basis of their anticipated contribution to the library of the three Ws: work, wisdom, and wealth. Let's look at this.

The library should elect members to its board who are willing to work at governing the library via policy enactment and oversight as well as roll up their sleeves when needed to help out, whether in soliciting funds or running a benefit. Trustees should also bring wisdom to the board by virtue of their experience and training. Board members should not only be knowledgeable about libraries but should possess management, financial, and human relations acumen. If you can get lawyers and accountants to serve on your board and share their knowledge, you are ahead of the game. As to "wealth," trustees do not have to be affluent and make big personal contributions to the library. However, they have to be willing and able to work at its funding, whether requesting tax funds from government or soliciting donations from businesses on Main Street. Small public libraries always do better at fund-raising when their board of trustees is actively involved and if they lead the way in giving.

CHAPTER ELEVEN

BUYING ON THE CHEAP

Living among the plain people in the Pennsylvania Dutch country, one absorbs some of the local values, and frugality is among those that we have accepted and applied to our library. Like the Ferengi on *Star Trek: Deep Space Nine*, we have developed our own "Rules of Acquisition":

1. Buy wholesale
2. Piggyback on government discount rates
3. Form or join in quantity purchase cooperatives
4. Exploit the Web
5. Compare prices and go beyond library suppliers
6. Use your tax exemption
7. Employ donations whenever you can

By applying these seven "rules," our library has been able to reduce its purchasing costs by 25 percent or more, thereby stretching our limited resources a bit further. Here is how we do it.

Buying Wholesale

The "buying wholesale" rule builds upon my New York City heritage, where the shopping cognoscenti know that smart people "never pay retail prices." We subscribe to this view in acquiring the things needed by our library, not just for books and AV materials but for our supplies as well.

Whenever possible, buy from wholesale, not retail, suppliers. By representing your library as a "business" to wholesale houses, they will be happy to sell to you at discounted rates of up to 50 percent off list price. We now buy at wholesale prices such commodities as office supplies, light bulbs, cleaning materials, restaurant supplies for our cooking classes, and even soap and toilet paper. Also consider shopping at "odd lot" closeout warehouses that deeply discount discontinued merchandise. Look into taking out a library membership in one or more of the "price clubs" such as Sam's Club, BJ's, or Costco.

Do not be shy about asking for "trade discounts" at vendors you may frequent. For example, I have found that many publishers, bookstores, and specialty book wholesalers will give up to 50 percent discounts to libraries if asked.

Piggybacking on Government Discount Rates

Government offices frequently negotiate "most favored buyer" quantity discounts with their suppliers. If your library receives support from a government agency, it too may be eligible to receive these discounted rates. My library is now eligible to purchase office supplies at county government rates and computer equipment at state government rates from a number of suppliers. In most cases you have only to tell the vendor you are a not-for-profit public library and ask for their government rate. This can save you thousands of dollars when purchasing big-ticket items such as computers, copiers, and software.

Make sure you take advantage of the federally supported Universal Services Fund (commonly known as E-Rate), which provides discounted voice, data, and Internet communications to schools and libraries. For more information on saving money through E-Rate, contact your state department of education or the U.S. Department of Education at http://www.ed.gov/Technology/eratemenu.html.

Participating in Quantity Purchasing Cooperatives

Join with other libraries in a purchasing cooperative and you can get your books and AV materials at maximum quantity discounts of up to 50 percent. Check with your county library, library district, or library system to determine if they have already set up central technical services operations to facilitate quantity purchasing and cataloging for a group of public libraries. Join with them if your needs and theirs are compatible. A byproduct of this type of cooperative acquisitions and cataloging is that it facilitates union catalogs and interlibrary loans among regional libraries. A cooperative can also usually get better rates in acquiring MARC/OCLC catalog records because it can contribute more original cataloging to offset purchases.

If you cannot find a cooperative library purchasing plan to join in your region, then consider banding together with other libraries to form one.

Exploiting the Web

Another good way to save money on library purchases is to buy on the Internet. The World Wide Web has evolved to the point where you can buy almost anything you need in your library from an online vendor, usually at a better price than you would pay in a store or from a catalog vendor. As many bargain hunters have learned, vendors of all sorts, from airlines to department stores, tend to offer their best discounts to online shoppers. For example, the January 2007 issue of *Consumer Reports* cites online vendor Amazon.com as offering discounts of 36 percent for online book purchases, more than triple the best discounts offered to the public in retail bookstores.

There is a range of modes to choose from when buying on the Web. Many manufacturers and retailers now offer direct e-sales online. There are auction-style services such as those offered by eBay, Froogle, and Yahoo. Fixed-price new and used books and other items are offered by online services such as Amazon.com, AbeBooks, Book-Finder, AddALL, and Alibris. When searching for a brand-name item, you may want to check one of the various "shopping bots" such as mySimon, PriceGrabber.com, BizRate, and others you can identify if you search the Web under "price compare." These bots will allow you to compare prices for a branded item among virtually all online vendors.

The principle of caveat emptor also applies to Internet buying. When buying on the Web (as when buying from a catalog), take into account the shipping and handling charges, because these can offset any savings. Buy from reliable vendors who guarantee their products, offer return privileges, and protect your confidential information (such as credit card data) using security systems such as VeriSign or PayPal. If buying on an online eBay-style auction, be sure to check the seller's references and avoid those with questionable histories.

Following these commonsense precautions, my library relies on the Web for many of its major or expensive purchases, including computer software and supplies, film for our passport camera, and name-brand kitchen equipment. In this way, we can regularly achieve discounts of 40–50 percent on our purchases. While we use a county library system cooperative for the lion's share of our book and AV material purchases, we buy many special, rush, and out-of-print replacement titles online from Amazon .com and Alibris at good prices with rapid delivery. We have built a respectable set of both current and classic feature films for our library by buying up "collections" of new and slightly used DVDs on eBay auctions, at about a tenth of what they sell for at retail.

Comparing Prices and Going beyond Library Suppliers

Public librarians who do not compare prices and who buy from only one library supplier may be spending more than they have to. Whether purchasing supplies, publications, or furniture, do seek competitive bids where feasible, or compare catalog prices. You can save 10 percent or more, which can mean a fair amount of dollars on major purchases.

For example, my public library along with most of the other ones in my county had traditionally been placing its periodical subscriptions through a well-known East

Coast national subscription agency at shallow or no discount. I received a flier in the mail from a small periodical jobber in the Midwest offering deep discounts and, out of curiosity, I asked it for a quotation on my list of about eighty titles. The firm offered me discounts of up to 20 percent per title and a more personalized level of service. I switched over to it three years ago and continue to enjoy the savings and service.

If you go beyond the traditional library supply houses when considering major purchases for items such as furniture, you might be surprised at the savings. You might find that you can buy similar items from "nonlibrary" sources at far lower prices. I learned this when my library received a $10,000 grant from a community foundation to purchase additional book stacks. However, in checking the prices of the traditional purveyors of library furniture, I found that my $10,000 was not enough to purchase all the additional shelving we needed. Out of necessity, I Googled the Web on the subject of "book shelves" and discovered a company in New England that manufactured shelving to order for bookstores. Its prices were 30 percent less than the library furniture suppliers. I checked out the company's references and installations at a couple of local bookshops and found that the shelves' style matched my needs and the quality was actually better than shelves we had previously purchased from traditional suppliers. As an additional benefit, these shelving units were delivered fully assembled and required no set-up labor. By shopping around and going beyond traditional library suppliers, we obtained more and paid less.

Using Your Tax Exemption

The Internal Revenue Service classifies most public libraries as paragraph 501(c)(3) not-for-profit tax-exempt organizations. As such, they are generally exempt from paying value-based taxes, including sales, real estate, and income taxes. Make sure you take advantage of your library's tax-exempt status in your purchases, because the money you save on taxes can be significant. You should also obtain a state tax-exempt license by applying to your state taxing agency. Generally, all you will need to do is to complete an application and attach a copy of your federal IRS 501(c)(3) classification letter. Some states may also ask for copies of your library's articles of incorporation and bylaws that declare it to be a not-for-profit organization.

Once you receive your state tax-exempt license, make a copy of it for every library staff member or trustee who purchases items on behalf of the library to use when they buy things. We provide wallet-sized copies that our managers carry around with them. In addition, it may be handy to set up tax-exempt corporate charge accounts with your major suppliers. In this way, the sales tax will be automatically omitted from all library orders.

Another advantage of having your IRS not-for-profit and tax-exempt credentials available is that they are often required as prerequisites to applying for certain grants.

Employing Donations

The cheapest way to acquire needed goods and services for your library is as a free donation, as mentioned previously. Do not be above soliciting donations of the things you need. Develop a "want" list of materials or assistance needed by the library and discreetly share it with your business community and government officials. They may have something you need as surplus that they would be pleased to share or donate.

For example, a local printer donates odd lots of surplus colored copy paper to us to use for posters and children's activities. A local manufacturing firm was cleaning out its warehouse and was able to donate some office desks and chairs that we needed. An insurance company was replacing its three-year-old computers and donated ten of the surplus machines to us to create a library computer laboratory. The borough road crew repaints the lines in our parking lot when they redo the lane markings on the road that goes by the library. Finally, if you elect a lawyer, an accountant, and a banker to your library board of trustees, you may be able to get free legal and financial advice.

CHAPTER TWELVE

CONCLUSION

Is It Worth All the Effort?

Five years ago, when I accepted a position as director of a small rural public library, I did so with mixed emotions. I had earned my M.S.L.S. "union card" at the (unfortunately now defunct) Columbia University School of Library Service, which was founded by Melvil Dewey and was arguably the most traditional library school in the United States. There I was steeped in the Carnegie tradition of the free public library serving as the "University of the People." Five years ago, however, a part of me now questioned whether the public library was still relevant in the fast-paced, electronic media-drenched twenty-first century. This concern became even more critical when I discovered how grossly underfunded (and underappreciated) my small public library was. In my darkest moment, I questioned my decision to become a public librarian and asked myself: "Why bother? Is it worth the effort? Do people care?"

Seeking an answer to these questions, I looked to the community to see if there was really any need for my public library in today's world. I discovered there indeed was. I found that certain "market segments" such as preschoolers, seniors, and new immigrants had nowhere else to go to satisfy their learning and information needs. I discovered latchkey kids in search of a wholesome, safe, "third place" refuge. I learned that the library, by default and necessity, is both a place to meet and a focal point for social and educational interaction.

They say that converts become the greatest zealots, and I guess that is what happened to me. Having been convinced that my public library had the potential to become the soul of the community, I dug in and drew upon my industry marketing experience. I exhorted my staff and volunteers to work with me to aggressively seek necessary funds for the library and then to use what resources we could get to provide responsive library services in a hospitable facility. When we had to, we used unconventional means toward our ends. Looking back, I ask, "Did our efforts pay off?"

Well, the community we serve is the only constituency qualified to vote on whether or not we have succeeded in offering them a high-quality public library that meets their needs. They vote with their feet. I guess the fact that our library's use statistics and level of support keep rising attests to some degree of patron satisfaction. Our library has also received some recognition and won a few awards. Therefore, maybe our efforts have not been in vain. We survived, we grew, and we had a heck of a lot of fun along the way.

As a born-again public library zealot, I can sincerely state to my colleagues in the 7,228 small public libraries of America that your communities need you and you serve an important and unique role. Because you are valuable, you must do what you have to not just to survive but also to flourish and excel.

I exhort those of you responsible for the survival of a small public library: do not be bashful in using the marketing and management techniques cited in the previous pages. Be passionate in reminding your community about the excellent work you do, and be aggressive in asking them for support. In this age of media hype, the public library now has to sell itself just like the churches, the universities, and even the government have learned to do. Try them and you might find that perhaps these marketing tools will work for you as they have worked for us. I truly believe that we small public libraries are still "the universities of the people." In an era of information overload and societal flux, we have a unique role as the information gatekeepers who offer a needed level of learning continuity by providing information delivery, validation, and discrimination. No other institution can do this for the population at large and for people of all ages, from infants to seniors. Our small public libraries are now at risk but are worth saving because we are still the only lifelong learning centers in town. Let us make sure that our constituents (and we) don't forget it!

May your small public library live long and prosper.

INSTITUTIONAL SOURCES
OF INFORMATION

One-Person Libraries

If you work in a one-person or small library, you might be interested in *OPL Plus* (http://opls.blogspot.com), a blog written by librarian and author Judith A. Siess, the author of *The OPL Sourcebook: A Guide for Solo and Small Libraries* (2001) and several other books. *OPL Plus* bills itself as a "blog for librarians in all smaller libraries, not just for one-person or solo librarians—all kinds of libraries, anywhere in the world. It offers management information, links, and marketing tips that you can use right now." The blog is library-focused yet eclectic and is a good resource for a solo librarian unable to monitor a lot of resource feeds.

The Association of Rural and Small Libraries and the Center for the Study of Rural Librarianship

In 1978 Bernard Vavrek of the Department of Library Science at the Clarion University of Pennsylvania organized a research facility known as the Center for the Study of Rural Librarianship (http://www.clarion.edu/rural/), which focused on public libraries in areas geographically isolated from metropolitan library systems. In addition to academic online instruction leading to a master's degree in rural and small libraries, the center conducts research, offers workshops, and maintains a publications program that includes the journals *Rural Libraries* and *Bookmobiles and Outreach Services*. In 2003 Clarion University helped to form the Association of Rural and Small Libraries (ARSL; see below), which holds joint annual meetings with the Association of Bookmobile and Outreach Services.

Provided below is a national and state-level resource guide for small and rural libraries that was distributed at the September 2006 Annual Meeting of the ARSL.

Small and Rural Libraries: National Resources

American Library Association, Office for Literacy and Outreach Services (http://www.ala.org/ala/olos/). This office supports and promotes literacy and equity of information access initiatives for traditionally underserved populations. These populations include new and nonreaders, people who are geographically isolated, people with disabilities, rural and urban poor people, and people generally discriminated against based on race, ethnicity, sexual orientation, age, language, or social class.

Association of Bookmobile and Outreach Services (http://abos.clarion.edu). Founded in 2004, its mission is to support and encourage government officials, library administrators, trustees, and staff in the provision of quality bookmobile and outreach services to meet diverse community information and programming needs. The association's electronic discussion list (abos-l@ clarion.edu) is available for members to share information and collaborate on topics of mutual interest. Included as well is chat functionality enabling members to discuss topics at the local or national level with their colleagues.

Association of Rural and Small Libraries (http://arsl.clarion.edu). Organized in 2003, this group includes all types of libraries—public, school, small urban branches, special and corporate, and small academic. Their defining characteristics are a limited budget and a diverse clientele. This movement comprises librarians, support staff, government officials, trustees, Friends of libraries, and professionals from other fields. The association's electronic discussion list (arsl@clarion.edu) is available for members to discuss mutual challenges and opportunities. Also included is a chat function enabling members to conduct their own local or regional discussions in addition to participating in national ones.

Cooperative State Research, Education, and Extension Service, U.S. Department of Agriculture (www.reeusda.gov). Best known as the Cooperative Extension Service, this resource is found in most of the counties of the United States. It is a natural ally for the local library. Its "Journal of Extension" provides vital reading to all who are interested in the ever-changing rural environment.

Economic Research Service, U.S. Department of Agriculture (www.ers.usda .gov). The premier agency providing data on rural America. Its publication *Rural America* (formerly *Rural Development Perspectives*) is required reading for understanding the socioeconomic conditions in rural areas.

ERIC Clearinghouse on Rural Education and Small Schools (http://www.ael.org/ eric/). Although no longer active, the website still provides a wide array of useful resources pertaining to rural, migrant, Mexican American, and small schools previously organized by the clearinghouse.

International Federation of Library Associations and Institutions, Mobile Libraries Section (http://www.ifla.org/VII/s38/ml.htm). An organization concerned with all aspects of mobile library operations, collections, services, education, and training, and research in all geographical areas.

Libri Foundation (www.librifoundation.org). A nationwide nonprofit organization that donates new, quality, hardcover children's books to small rural public libraries in the United States through its Books for Children program.

National Agricultural Library, Rural Information Center (http://www.nal.usda.gov/ric/). Provides information and referral services to local, state, federal, and tribal government officials; community organizations; rural electric and telephone cooperatives; libraries; businesses; and citizens working to maintain the vitality of America's rural areas. Additionally, its services include a wide variety of links to other rural-related resources, including the ever-interesting question "What is rural?"

National Center for Education Statistics, Library Statistics Program (http://nces.ed.gov/surveys/libraries/public.asp). This is the single most important resource for the study of rural and small library culture in the United States. Data on the smallest library unit are provided. The NCES also provides the Public Library Peer Comparison Tool and the Public Library Locator for contrasting similarities and differences among libraries.

Regional Centers for Rural Development: Northeast Regional Center for Rural Development, Southern Rural Development Center, North Central Regional Center for Rural Development, and Western Rural Development Center. These five centers make up a network of institutions conducting research, providing continuing education, contributing publications, and providing other services to those interested in rural America. The U.S. Department of Agriculture, land-grant universities, and other institutions support the regional centers.

Rural Library Project. A not-for-profit organization committed to the establishment of new small libraries in rural areas. Provides project management services and grants. Contact: Dan White, dwhite@rurallibraryproject.org, 404-377-5878.

WebJunction Rural Library Sustainability Project (http://webjunction.org/do/navigation?category=13496). Funded by the Bill and Melinda Gates Foundation, this project provides training grants to develop a community of interest around sustainability, technology, and advocacy for small and rural libraries. It provides monthly webinars. Contact: Jim Malzewski, malzewsj@oclc.org, 206-273-7522.

Small and Rural Libraries: Resources by State

Arizona State Library, Archives and Public Records (http://www.dlapr.lib.az.us/cdt/intro.htm). Online course in collection development.

California Rural Library Resource Clearinghouse (www.resourceroundup.net). Contact: Carla Lehn, clehn@library.ca.gov, 916-653-7743.

California State Library, Rural Library Initiative (www.rurallibraries.org). A variety of resources to assist rural libraries.

Florida Library Association, Small and Rural Libraries Interest Group. Contact: Ron Moore, moore@lakeline.lib.fl.us, 352-669-1001.

Idaho Commission for Libraries (http://www.lili.org/forlibs/ce/). Online courses in basic library education.

Illinois State Library, Small Public Library Management Institute (http://www.cyberdriveillinois.com/departments/library/whats_new/2006splmi.html).

Indiana Library Federation, Small and Medium Size Libraries Division. 2007 conference chair: Sally Stegner, sistegne@lpld.lib.in.us, 812-537-2775.

Iowa State Library Association, Iowa Small Library Association. Chair: Elaine Reitz, ereitz@north-liberty.lib.ia.us, 319-626-5701.

Library of Michigan. Holds rural library conferences. Contact: Deb Bacon-Ziegler, bacon-ziegler@michigan.gov, 517-373-3746.

Michigan Library Association, Rural and Small Libraries Roundtable. Chair: Ryan Wieber, rwieber@otseqolibrary.org, 269-694-6455.

Minnesota Library Association, Small and Rural Libraries Round Table. Chair: Robin Chaney, robin@sammie.org, 507-532-9013.

Missouri State Library (http://www.sos.mo.gov/library/development/summer institute2006/). Holds summer institute.

Nevada State Library and Archives, Nevada Library Institute. Holds rural library workshops. Contact: Holly Van Valkenburgh, hvanvalk@clan.lib.nv.us, 775-684-3322.

New Hampshire Library Association, Small Libraries Section. Contact: Doris Mitton, daltonpl@ncia.net, 603-837-2751.

New Jersey Library Association, Small Libraries Section. Contact: Pat Tumulty, ptumulty@njla.org, 609-394-8032.

Ohio Library Council, Small Libraries Division. Provides online training, conferences, publications, and an electronic discussion list. Chair: James Wilkins, wilkinji@oplin.org, 419-562-7327.

South Dakota State Library, Library Training Institute (http://www.sdstatelibrary.com/forlibrarians/institute/index.htm). Provides a four-year training program for small and medium-sized public library staff and trustees.

Tennessee State Library and Archives, Tennessee Public Library Management Institute (http://www.tennessee.gov/tsla/lps/plmi/plmi.htm).

Texas Library Association, Small Community Libraries Round Table. Publishes a newsletter at http://www.txla.org/groups/pdf/sclrtssummer04.pdf. Chair: Joyce Trent, librarian@leonvalley.lib.tx.us, 210-684-0720.

Texas State Library, Small Library Management Training Program (http://www.tsl.state.tx.us/ld/projects/slmtp/index.html).

Utah State Library (http://library.utah.gov/library_services/continuing_education/basic_skills_courses.htm). Provides online basic skills courses.

West Virginia Library Commission (http://librarycommission.lib.wv.us). Provides online seminars. Contact: Rebecca Van Der Meer, vandermr@wvlc.libwv.us, 800-642-9021, extension 2011.

Wisconsin Library Association, Wisconsin Small Libraries Round Table. Chair: Janean Miller, jmiller@swis.org, 608-375-5723.

SAMPLE SURVEY QUESTIONS

Formal Questionnaire

Do you use the library?

    If no, why not?

Do you use other information services?

    Which ones?

How do you use the library?

    Personal visit

    Telephone

    Online

How often do you use the library?

    Daily

    Weekly

    Biweekly

    Other _____

What information do you access at the library?

    Books

    Periodicals

    Online workstations

    Reference questions

    A quiet place to do work

What topics does your library use involve?

Critical Incident Questionnaire Format

The last time you visited the library, what information did you find?

    Were you happy with what you found?

    Why?

Focus Interview Format

What information do you use in your
> Work?
> Hobby?
> Recreation?

How and where do you usually find this information?

Do you use the library?
> How?

How do you feel about the library?
> Why?

SAMPLE DIRECT MAIL SOLICITATION LETTER AND DONOR REPLY CARD

MILANOF-SCHOCK LIBRARY
1184 Anderson Ferry Road
Mount Joy, PA 17552
717-653-1510 I fax: 717-653-6590
www.mslibrary.org

Serving East Donegal Township, Marietta Borough, Mount Joy Borough,
Mount Joy Township, and Rapho Township

March 2006

> "The Milanof-Schock Library is a shining example of small libraries throughout the country that, despite scarce resources and growing, diverse service areas, are providing critical learning and networking opportunities to their patrons and helping create stronger, more vital communities in the process."
>
> > *Martha Choe, director of the Bill and Melinda Gates Global Libraries Program, February 2006. In recognition of Milanof-Schock being named the Best Small Library in America, 2006.*

Dear Milanof-Schock Library Patron:

Your community library has just been named the Best Small Library in America by *Library Journal* and the Bill and Melinda Gates Foundation. Since the monies we receive from municipalities, the county, and the state cover only about 48 percent of our operating expenses, we could not have provided the high-quality services and programs that qualified us for the award without our patrons' financial support in 2005.

It is now time for our 2006 Library fund drive.

Will you please enable us to continue to provide you and your family with the quality of community library service you deserve? Although we do our best to reduce costs and to raise money through book sales, auctions, and other means, we still need your donations to continue our programs.

We know that you appreciate the Library's services and want them to continue. Your tax-deductible gift will help make that possible. Please complete the enclosed card and mail it with your contribution in the pre-addressed envelope or deposit it at the library.

Thank you in advance for your consideration and generous gift.

Sincerely,

Deborah Owens
President of the Board

Board of Directors

Deborah Owens, President | Carl Hallgren, Vice President | Patricia Eicherly, Treasurer | Cheryl Deck, Corresponding Secretary | Linda Good | Bernerd Grissinger | Lilli Ann Kopp | Marianne Melleby

Staff and Volunteer Leaders

Herbert Landau, Director | Nancy Behney, Assistant Director | Susan Craine, Technical Services Coordinator | Greta Kerniky, Community Relations Coordinator | Janet Betty, Children's Coordinator | Donna Little, Volunteer Coordinator | Judy Bard | Diane Creveling | Jody Crowe | Carol Miller | Stacy Emminger | Lora Jones, Friends President

Annual Appeal 2006–2007

❏ Business   ❏ Family/Individual   Date: _____

Contribution

❏ $25   ❏ $50   ❏ $75   ❏ $100   ❏ $250   ❏ $500   ❏ $1,000   ❏ $5,000
❏ Other _____

Please make check out to Milanof-Schock Library

Charge card donations

❏ Visa   ❏ Mastercard
Card number_____ Exp.: _____
Name on card: _____
Signature: _____

Credit card payments also may be made online at www.mslibrary.org

❏ I am enclosing a matching gift form
❏ I would like to donate appreciated stock or bonds (call our treasurer
at 717-653-1510)

Name _____

Address _____

_____

Phone _____

E-mail _____

❏ I wish to remain anonymous
❏ I would like a receipt
❏ I would like to serve as a library volunteer

MILANOF-SCHOCK LIBRARY
1184 Anderson Ferry Road
Mount Joy, PA 17552
717-653-1510 I fax: 717-653-6590
www.mslibrary.org

HOW TO EVALUATE AND DESCRIBE
OLD AND RARE BOOKS

What's My Book Worth?
A Brief Guide to Evaluating and Describing Old and Rare Books

Courtesy of the Public Services Division
of the State Library of Pennsylvania
www.statelibrary.state.pa.us

The State Library does not offer appraisal services, but has put together this brief guide to help you evaluate and describe old and rare books. Remember that library personnel are here to serve you as an information resource and offer many materials from our various collections, as well as public access to the Internet.

How to Describe an Old Book

There are at least eight facts a book dealer needs to know about your book:

1. Author (last name first)
2. Title of the Book
3. Place of Publication (items 3, 4, and 5 may be on the title page or reverse of title page)
4. Publisher
5. Date of Publication
6. Size (height of book)
7. Kind of Binding (cloth, leather, etc.)
8. Condition of Book (see list of industry standards below)

Industry Standards

It is important to both collectors and dealers that you accurately describe your book's condition using industry standards.

As New is to be used only when the book is in the same immaculate condition in which it was published. There can be no defects, no missing pages, no library stamps, etc., and the dust jacket (if issued with one) must be perfect, without any tears. (The term *As New* is preferred over the alternative term *Mint* to describe a copy that is perfect in every respect, including jacket.)

Fine approaches the condition of *As New*, but without being crisp. For the use of the term *Fine* there must also be no defects, etc. If the jacket has a small tear or looks worn, this must be noted.

Very Good can describe a used book that does show some small signs of wear—but no tears—on either binding or paper. Any defects must be noted.

Good describes the average used and worn book that has all pages or leaves present. Any defects must be noted.

Fair describes a worn book that has complete text pages, including those with maps or plates, but may lack endpapers, half title, etc., which must be noted. Binding, jacket (if any), etc., may also be worn. All defects must be noted.

Poor describes a book that is sufficiently worn that its only merit is as a Reading Copy because it does have the complete text, which must be legible. Any missing maps or plates should still be noted. This copy may be soiled, scuffed, stained, or spotted, and may have loose joints, hinges, pages, etc.

Ex-Library copies must always be designated as such, *no matter what the condition of the book.*

Book Club editions must always be noted as such, *no matter what the condition of the book.*

Binding Copy describes a book in which the pages or leaves are perfect, but the binding is very bad, loose, off, or nonexistent.

Dust Jacket. In all cases, the lack of a dust jacket should be noted if the book was issued with one. If the book has a dust jacket, save it. Even if torn, the book's value is enhanced by it.

Foxed or Foxing describes rust-brown discoloration of the paper.

Rebound describes a book that is not bound in original binding.

Uncut Edges means that the edges of a book are untrimmed by machinery; and *Unopened* means that the untrimmed edges have not been opened by hand.

Autographed. If a book has been signed by the author, it is important to note this.

Repaired. Describe what has been repaired.

An example of a description prepared using industry standards:

Scott, Joseph. A Geographical Description of Pennsylvania, Philadelphia, Cochran, 1806. 5 1/2 inches, leather, Good, with original dust jacket.

Where to Go for Information

You can get a general indication of the value of your book by consulting the following references. Note that this list is not all-inclusive, but provides you with a starting point in your quest. The rare book trade is subject to fluctuating values based upon collector interest, availability, condition of the book, and of course, supply and demand.

REFERENCE BOOKS

> *American Book Prices* (Leab)
> *Collected Books: The Guide to Values 1998* (Ahern)
> *Used Book Price Guide* (Mandeville)
> *A Handbook for Book Lovers* (LaFontaine)
> *Bookman's Price Index* (McGrath)
> *Book Prices: Used and Rare* (Zempel and Verkler)

WEBSITES

> Antiquarian Booksellers Association of America, www.abaa.org
> Bibliofind, www.bibliofind.com
> BookFinder, www.bookfinder.com

SAMPLE HONOR/
MEMORIAL GIFT FORM

MILANOF-SCHOCK LIBRARY
1184 Anderson Ferry Road
Mount Joy, PA 17552
717-653-1510
www.mslibrary.org

**YOU CAN HONOR LOVED ONES OR REMEMBER THE DEPARTED
WITH A BOOK AT THE MILANOF-SCHOCK LIBRARY.**

RECOGNIZE FAMILY, FRIENDS, TEACHERS, AND OTHERS WHO HAVE TOUCHED YOUR LIFE.

Our honor and memorial book plan allows you to honor or remember a family member, friend, or a special individual in a lasting way. You can make a tax-deductible contribution of $25 or more for a book to be presented to the library in the name of a friend, relative, or special person. You may return the attached form with a payment to the Library.

Library staff will select a new book and include in it a bookplate giving the name of the donor and the person being honored or remembered. You can request a book on a special subject or by a special author. An acknowledgment letter identifying the donor will also be sent to the person or the family of the person being honored or remembered.

I wish to make a donation of $_____ for a book to be placed in the Milanof-Schock Library:

In Honor/Memory of

Name _____

❑ Memorial

❑ Anniversary

❑ Graduation

❑ Birthday

❑ Other (please specify) _____

Recommended Book Subject, Type, or Author (optional)

_____

The library will make every effort to consider your recommendation, but reserves the right to make the final decision.

Name of Donor _____

Address _____

_____

Phone _____

E-mail _____

Relationship to Honoree _____

Recipient Information (optional)
(An acknowledgment will be sent to this person.)

Recipient's Name _____

Address _____

_____

Phone _____

Relationship to Honoree _____

Bookplate Samples
(Actual bookplate may look different.)

In Honor of

Presented by

Date

In Memory of

Presented by

Date

SAMPLE CUSTOM RESEARCH LETTER
CONTRACT AGREEMENT AND FORMS

Note: This example is not meant to be legal advice. Review final documents with your attorney to ensure that they comply with all applicable regulations and codes.

Sample Research Contract

This represents an agreement between (client name) authorizing the XYZ Public Library to perform the following service(s) on a time and materials fee basis: _____ _____. These services are to be conducted in the time period _____ to _____. Research projects are billed only in increments of one hour.

The fee(s) for these services will be ____/hour and ____/page plus out-of-pocket expenses. Normal turnaround time is the turnaround time for Standard service ($75/ hour) and is approximately two weeks.

(The next paragraph is optional.)

The total cost for this engagement is not to exceed $_____ without prior client written authorization. Monthly current awareness searches can be arranged at $_____/month. Billing will be on a monthly basis.

The scope of this engagement will be as defined on the attached Custom Library Services Request Form.

The library reserves the right to assign qualified staff (and subcontractors [optional]) at its sole discretion.

All work done by XYZ Public Library will be done in a confidential manner. While XYZ Public Library attempts to provide accurate information, it makes no warranties, and disclaims any liability for loss or damage to any party caused by errors or omissions or statements of any kind.

The XYZ Public Library does not perform research for student assignments or papers and does not provide legal, medical, tax, or accounting advice.

Either party to this agreement may unilaterally terminate the engagement with seven days notice.

Signed:

Client _____ Date _____

XYZ Public Library _____ Date _____

❐ Credit Card   ❐ VISA   ❐ MasterCard   ❐ American Express

Card # _____ Expires _____

❐ Cash on personal pick-up

Sample Request Form for Custom Information Research

Please fill out the form below. Once we receive it, someone will contact you about your request and payment information.

Client Information

Name _____

Title _____

Company Name _____

Street Address _____

City/State _____

ZIP Code _____

Phone _____

Fax _____

E-mail _____

Information Request

Please describe the information you are looking for. Be as specific and detailed as possible. Please briefly describe your research topic. Include any limits to your topic such as years to be covered. Describe any other restrictions. For example: money or time limits for delivery of the research.

_____

_____

_____

_____

Supplementary Information

Please provide the following information:

Special terms, key words, known names, publications, and cross-references:

_____

Is it possible to limit years and geographic regions of the search?   ❑ Yes ❑ No

What are your expectations for the volume of information? _____

In what format do you envision the final product?   ❑ Study ❑ Database
❑ Web page ❑ Bibliography ❑ Other _____

When do you need the results of the custom research completed? _____

Do you have any other background information?_____

If you have done any preliminary work, please describe it briefly so that time will
not be spent on work already completed. _____

Describe other restrictions that might be pertinent to the researcher.

_____

Search question: (Please give a detailed statement in your own words, defining
relationships and giving synonyms. Do not just give key words.) _____

Databases to be searched: _____

Years to be searched: _____

Limits. Please check all that apply: ❑ English only
❑ Other languages (please specify) _____

Delivery and Payment

Print format:

_____ Citation only (author, title, source, accession number)

_____ Citation and abstract

_____ All fields (author, title, source, abstract, mesh headings, etc.)

How do you prefer your research to be sent to you? Choose one of the following:

❐ Fax   ❐ Courier   ❐ Mail   ❐ E-mail   ❐ Will pick up

How would you like to pay for this service?

❐ Cash or Check   ❐ Invoice
❐ Invoicing available to companies and organizations

Price limit: What is the maximum you are willing to pay for this service? _____

Date needed: _____

Please note that certain time limits may not allow for comprehensive research. The turnaround time for Standard service ($75/hour) is approximately two weeks. All projects due within three to ten business days are billed at the Rush rate ($90/hour). Those due within two business days are billed at the Expedited Rush rate ($125/hour).

PRESS RELEASE GUIDELINES
AND SAMPLE PRESS RELEASE

Press Release Formatting Guidelines

Contact Information

Indicate who the reporter should contact for more information or to arrange an interview or photo shoot. Include name, address, title, phone and e-mail, and library name and website URL.

Headline

The headline is one of the most important components of the press release because it needs to "grab the attention" of the editor. It should be in bold type and a font that is larger than the body text. Preferred type fonts are Arial, Times New Roman, or Verdana. Keep the headline to 80–125 characters in one sentence. Capitalize the first letter of every word with the exception of "a," "the," "an," or any word that is three characters or less. Omit exclamation marks ("!"); they only sell your release as advertising, not as news.

Summary

Give the city, state, month, day, and year. Your summary paragraph should be written in a clear and concise manner. The opening sentence contains the most important information; keep it to 25 words or less. Never take for granted that the reader has read your headline. Write a comprehensive summary of your press release that helps clarify the headline and describes what the press release is about. If pressed for space, the summary is all that a reporter may use, so make sure that it tells the whole story in abbreviated format.

Body (Answer the Who, What, Where, When, Why, and How)

The body of your release can be more than one paragraph, but try to keep the press release under 400 words total. Additional paragraphs should contain supporting information and statistics. Remember, succinct and to the point works best. Your story must be newsworthy and factual. Don't make it a sales pitch or it will end up in the trash.

LEAD PARAGRAPH (ANSWER THE WHO, WHAT, WHERE, WHEN, WHY, AND HOW)

Provide the full names of your organization and any involved individual's names, affiliations, and titles. Beginning with a strong introductory paragraph captures the reader's attention and contains the information most relevant to your message. Cover the basics of who, what, where, when, why, and how. This paragraph should present an informative abstract of the entire press release and include a hook to get your audience interested in reading more.

SECOND PARAGRAPH (ANSWER THE WHY AND HOW)

The second paragraph of the body should connect the first paragraph to more detailed information about the "why" and the "how" of the news event.

ADDITIONAL PARAGRAPHS (AMPLIFICATION AND QUOTES)

Additional paragraphs should contain more detailed information and make up the body of the release. Pick up with the information provided in your first paragraph, including quotes from key staff, patrons, donors, or subject matter experts. Make sure you use correct grammar so as not to affect your credibility negatively.

It is good form to include at least one quote from a library official or grant agency executive or library patron that states why this is an important news event. To add credibility to your press release, identify the people you quote using their title and employer name in addition to their full name. Make sure you are cleared to use quotes, photographs, or information about other organizations or individuals. Have an angle that will appeal to journalists (try connecting your release to current events or issues with an emphasis on human interest). Effective releases utilize a strategy known as the inverted pyramid, with the most important information and quotes first.

About (Institutional Background Summary)

Include a brief description of your library along with the services it provides, its hours, and location. You may also include background on other organizations and individuals cited in the release.

Final Paragraph (Call to Action)

Restate and summarize the key points of your release and provide a call to action. This is your opportunity to prompt your target audience to do something. Provide a pointer to additional information by stating: "For additional information on [the subject of this release], contact [name], or visit www.yoururl.com." If you offer a sample, copy, or demo, put that information in here. You can also include details on reservations, fees, and other conditions in this area of the release. If your release goes over one page, type "MORE" at the bottom of the first page and number your pages. If you have attachments, such as photos, add a note: "PHOTO ATTACHED."

End

Signify the end of the release by either three pound signs ("###") or the word "END" on the first line after your text is completed. This lets the journalists know they have received the entire release.

A FINAL NOTE: With an effective release, it should be possible to cut off at the end of any paragraph and still provide journalists with sufficient information. This is known as allowing for "get-off points."

Sample Press Release

LIBRARY NEWS NOTES
For more information contact:
Grant Winner, Community Relations Coordinator

MILANOF-SCHOCK LIBRARY
1184 Anderson Ferry Road
Mount Joy, PA 17552
717-653-1510 I fax: 717-653-6590
www.mslibrary.org
E-mail: winner@mountjoy.lib.pa.us

Milanof-Schock Library Named 2006 Best Small Library in America

Mount Joy, PA, February 1, 2006—From a field of over 50 nominations nationwide, *Library Journal* has selected the Milanof-Schock Library in Mount Joy, Pennsylvania, for the annual Best Small Library in America Award. Cosponsored by the Bill and Melinda Gates Foundation, the award was founded to encourage and showcase exemplary work of libraries serving populations under 25,000. *Library Journal* editors and a panel of national library leaders selected the Milanof-Schock Library for its tremendous commitment to its community, and its ever-expanding services.

First started in 1962 as a project of the Girl Scouts, the Milanof-Schock Library (MSL) has become an integral part of its community. The only library serving the 20,000 residents in its 50-square-mile district, the Milanof-Schock Library balances the needs of a diverse audience serving many faiths, including a large Amish population and an expansive farming community in the second-largest agricultural producing county in the United States.

"The story of MSL is the story of squeezing a great deal of library service out of $10.86 a head. It is the story of finding new, creative ways to be the center of a geographically expansive area, a deeply conservative and religious yet very diverse community. It is the story of building a library and a service to fit the needs of a place and the people who pay for it, partly in cash freely given and partly through taxes. It is the story of the Best Small Library in America 2006," remarked John Berry III, editor in chief, *Library Journal*, who wrote the February 1, 2006, cover story that announces the winner. (The article is also available at www.libraryjournal.com.)

Martha Choe, director of the Bill and Melinda Gates Global Libraries Program, praised the library, stating, "The Milanof-Schock Library is a shining example of small libraries throughout the country that, despite scarce resources and growing, diverse service areas, are providing critical learning and networking opportunities to their patrons and helping create stronger, more vital communities in the process."

Deborah Owens, the president of the Milanof-Schock Library's Board, stated, "The library's success comes from several sources: a Board of Trustees that respects each other and works together for the library, a warm and caring staff and management team who are committed to providing top-quality service to the community, and an energetic and committed director who works tirelessly on grants and upgrading our services. We are also indebted to the Friends of the Library, community citizens, and municipalities for their financial support."

The library provides a variety of programs and has expanded its offerings from 5 to 50 per month to meet the demands of its community:

- The library boasts the "Reads on Wheels" program, delivering books and AV materials to 200 homebound individuals.

- The library provides working space for two groups of the Society of Farmwives, comprising women who are the de facto business managers of their farms, to meet and solve problems together.

- The library acts as a building ground to foster new relationships between the community and newly arrived immigrant families. It started a Culture and Cooking series, which invites new immigrants to share their culture and cuisine with the community.

- The library also acts as the meeting place for the local Chamber of Commerce, Mount Joy Police Department, and other businesses, clubs, and societies.

The library also hosts a robust public-access computing program. It currently has 30 computers available for public access, 10 purchased with a grant from the Bill and Melinda Gates Foundation and 10 donated by the Highmark Blue Shield. The library has a $46,000 Library Services and Technology Act grant and a ten-course syllabus. The library has partnered with Pennsylvania State University to evaluate its education programs and help with grant applications for additional programs.

With a small staff of only two full-timers and about 20 volunteers, the Milanof-Schock Library relies on grants, book sales, and donations to sustain its collections, building, programs, and services. About 48 percent of the library's annual budget comes from state, county, and local government. Library director Herb Landau and the Milanof-Schock Library board raise 52 percent of the library's operating funds, primarily through community fund-raisers and foundations. The library's annual benefit auction provides $15,000 a year, over $20,000 comes from library book sales, $20,000 comes from an annual direct mail plea to individuals and businesses, and local businesses donate over $15,000 each year. The library also receives revenue by lending space to the U.S. State Department Passport Application Agency and earning $30 per passport that it issues.

As the winner of the 2006 Best Small Library in America, the Milanof-Schock Library will receive a $10,000 award, and conference costs for two library representatives to attend the March 2006 Public Library Association meeting and gala reception where the library will be honored.

About the Milanof-Schock Library

The library, located in Mount Joy, serves the Donegal School District and the municipalities of East Donegal Township, Marietta Borough, Mount Joy Borough, Mount Joy Township, and Rapho Township. The number of patrons that the library serves has grown steadily. In 2005 the library served 71,559 visitors with over 148,000 items circulated. The library adds about 100 new library cardholders each month.

The Milanof-Schock Library began library service to residents of the Donegal area of Lancaster County in 1962 as a Girl Scout troop community project. A bookmobile stop was established in a former storefront on Main Street in Mount Joy in 1964. When the library outgrew its storefront, a major capital fund drive began in 1996. Two major gifts totaling over $800,000 were received from the estate of Mount Joy resident Anne Milanof and from the SICO Foundation, in memory of Clarence Schock, the founder of Schock Independent Oil Company (SICO). These two bequests funded a new building that opened in 1999 and was designated the Milanof-Schock Library

A fully accessible, 12,000-square-foot building holds a collection of over 27,000 items, including books, audiovisual materials, and periodicals. There is also free computer and Internet access, as well as computers for children with educational and recreational games. The library also has an extensive and diverse educational program schedule for children, youth, and adults.

The Milanof-Schock Library currently employs 2 full-time staff, 7 part-time employees, and 20 active volunteers. The library director is Herb Landau.

About Library Journal

Founded by Melvil Dewey in 1876, *Library Journal* is the oldest and most respected publication covering the library field and is read by over 100,000 librarians nationwide. *Library Journal* is an independent voice dedicated to reporting for and about the library field.

About the Bill and Melinda Gates Foundation

The Bill and Melinda Gates Foundation works to promote greater equity in four areas: global health, education, public libraries, and support for at-risk families in Washington State and Oregon. The Seattle-based foundation joins local, national, and international partners to ensure that advances in these areas reach those who need them most. Cochairs Bill Gates, Melinda Gates, and William H. Gates Sr. and CEO Patty Stonesifer lead the foundation.

To celebrate the Best Small Library award, the Milanof-Schock Library invites all county residents to an Open House to be held on Sunday, April 2, from 2:00 p.m. to 4:00 p.m. at the Library in Mount Joy. There will be light refreshments and music by a string quartet. See and experience what makes the Milanof-Schock Library the

"Best Small Library in America 2006." The Milanof-Schock Library is located at 1184 Anderson Ferry Road, Mount Joy. For more information, call 717-653-1510 or visit www.mslibrary.org.

For the online *Library Journal* article on the award, go to www.libraryjournal .com, February 2006 issue, "Everyone's Hitching Post—Best Small Library in America 2006."

For more information, please contact:

Herbert Landau, Milanof-Schock Library: 717-653-1510, landau@mountjoy .lib.pa.us

John Berry, *Library Journal:* 203-359-2495, jberry@reedbusiness.com

Allison Davis, the Bill and Melinda Gates Foundation: 206-352-8598 or media@ gatesfoundation.org

(### END)

SAMPLE BYLAWS FOR A FRIENDS OF THE LIBRARY GROUP

BYLAWS OF THE FRIENDS OF THE MILANOF-SCHOCK LIBRARY

I. Name

>   The name of this organization shall be The Friends of the Milanof-Schock Library.

II. Purpose

>   The purpose of the Friends shall be to maintain an association of persons interested in the growth and development of libraries; to focus attention on library services, facilities, and needs; and to stimulate contributions through projects and special events.

III. Membership and Dues

>   A. The membership of this organization shall include any individual who has paid the annual dues. All such persons shall be considered voting members and are entitled to hold office.

>   B. Annual dues, as designated by the Board of Directors, shall be paid by members in January.

>   C. Any increase in the annual dues must be approved by a majority of the Board of Directors.

IV. Finance

>   A. Fiscal Year

>   The fiscal year of this organization shall begin on January 1.

>   B. Depositories and Disbursements

>   1. All funds shall be deposited to the account of the Friends of the Milanof-Schock Library and shall be disbursed by the treasurer as authorized by the Executive Board.

>   2. This corporation is organized and operated exclusively for charitable purposes within the meaning of section 501(c)(3) of the Internal Revenue Code.

3. No part of the net earnings of the organization shall inure to the benefit of, or be distributable to its members, trustees, officers, or other private persons. No substantial part of the activities of the organization shall be the carrying on of propaganda, or otherwise attempting to influence legislation, and the organization shall not participate in or intervene in (including the publishing or distribution of statements) any political campaign on behalf of any candidate for public office.

4. Notwithstanding any other provision of these Articles, the corporation shall not carry on any other activities not permitted to be carried on (a) by a corporation exempt from federal income tax under section 501(c)(3) of the Internal Revenue Code of 1986 (or the corresponding provision of any future United States Internal Revenue Law) or (b) by a corporation, contributions to which are deductible under section 170(c)(2) of the Internal Revenue Code of 1986 (or the corresponding provision of any future United States Internal Revenue Law.)

5. Upon winding up and dissolution of this corporation, after paying or adequately providing for the debts and obligations of the corporation, the remaining assets shall be distributed to a non-profit fund, foundation, or corporation which is organized and operated exclusively for charitable, educational, religious, and/or scientific purposes and which has established its tax exempt status under section 501(c)(3) of the Internal Revenue Code.

C. The Board of Directors shall provide for such audit and control of its funds as are necessary for their safekeeping and complete accounting at the end of the fiscal year.

V. Audit

The financial records will be audited yearly by an independent person.

VI. Officers

A. There shall be a president, vice-president, secretary, and treasurer.

B. Duties

1. President

a. Preside at all meetings of the Friends.

b. Call special meeting of the Board in accordance with provisions of the Bylaws.

c. Appoint chairpersons of all committees except the nominating committee.

d. Serve as ex-officio member of all committees except the nominating committee.

  e. As necessary, attend meetings of the Library Board of Directors as a nonvoting member.

  f. As necessary, appoint a member to be historian.

 2. Vice-President

  a. Preside at all meetings in the absence or disability of the President.

  b. Perform such other duties as requested by the President or the Board.

 3. Secretary

  a. Record and keep the minutes of all meetings of the Friends, and report same to the Friends for approval at their next meeting.

  b. Have available for reference at all meetings a copy of the Bylaws and a list of the officers and committee chairpersons.

  c. Handle all official correspondence and communications.

 4. Treasurer

  a. Collect and assume responsibility of contributions and funds received.

  b. Disburse funds (pay bills).

  c. Present financial report to the Board at its regular meeting.

  d. Present annual financial statement at the end of each fiscal year.

  e. Present books annually to an independent auditor.

C. Election and Tenure

 1. Nominations

  a. Each August, a nominating committee of not less than three (3) shall be appointed by the board for a one (1) year term.

  b. The chairman shall be determined by the committee.

  c. At the October meeting, the committee shall present to the membership a single slate of nominees.

  d. Nominations may be made from the floor at the time of the election, provided the personal or written consent of the nominee has been secured.

 2. Election

  a. Voting shall be by ballot at the November meeting.

  b. All officers shall be on the slate.

  c. All officers shall take office at the January meeting.

3. Tenure

> The president, vice-president, secretary, and treasurer shall all serve a one (1) year term.

4. Vacancies

> In case of any vacancy in office, the vice-president shall succeed the president, and any other vacancy shall be filled for the remainder of the term through appointment by the Executive Committee.

VII. Meetings and Quorums

A. Regular meetings of the Board of Directors may be held four (4) times per year at a time and place designated by the Board.

B. Regular meetings of the membership will be held ten (10) times per year at the library.

C. Special meetings may be held at a time and place designated by the President. Only business for which notice to the membership has been given shall be transacted.

VIII. Board of Directors and Executive Committee

A. Board of Directors

1. The Board of Directors shall be composed of the officers, chairpersons of standing committees, project chairpersons, and the immediate past-president.

2. The Board of Directors shall carry on the business of the organization.

3. A majority of the membership of the Board of Directors shall constitute a quorum.

B. Executive Committee

1. The Executive Committee shall be composed of the elected officers and the immediate past-president.

2. Duties: (a) Empowered to elect additional members, as needed, to constitute a board for the effective operation of the organization; (b) Emergency power to act for the Board between meetings of the Board.

3. Meetings of the Executive Committee shall be held on the call of the President or two (2) members of the Executive Committee.

4. A majority of the Executive Committee shall constitute a quorum.

IX. Committees

The President shall be empowered to appoint any special or standing committees deemed advisable.

X.   Amendments to the Bylaws

Provisions of these Bylaws may be amended by a two-third vote of the Board of Directors at any regular or special meeting provided that notice of the proposed amendment shall have been given to all members in writing at least two (2) weeks before the said meeting.

These Bylaws were revised, voted on, and approved by the membership of the Milanof-Schock Library Friends on March 13, 2006.

SELECTED BIBLIOGRAPHY

Fund-Raising

Baker and Taylor Company. *Winning the Money Game: A Guide to Community-Based Library Fundraising*. New York: Baker and Taylor, 1979.

Bonnell, Pamela G. *Fund Raising for the Small Library*. Chicago: American Library Association, 1983.

Burlingame, Dwight F., ed. *Library Fundraising: Models for Success*. Chicago: American Library Association, 1995.

Daubert, Madeline J. *Financial Management for Small and Medium-Sized Libraries*. Chicago: American Library Association, 1993.

Falkenstein, J. A. *National Guide to Funding for Libraries and Information Services*. New York: Foundation Center, 2003.

Herring, Mark Youngblood. *Raising Funds with Friends Groups*. New York: Neal-Schuman, 2004.

Hill, Malcolm K. *Budgeting and Financial Record Keeping in the Small Library*. Chicago: American Library Association, 1993.

Lynch, Mary Jo. *Non-Tax Sources of Revenue for Public Libraries*. Chicago: American Library Association, 1989.

Martin, Murray S., and Betsy Park. *Charging and Collecting Fees and Fines: A Handbook for Libraries*. New York: Neal-Schuman, 1998.

Rosenberg, Philip. *Cost Finding for Public Libraries: A Manager's Handbook*. Chicago: American Library Association, 1985.

Steele, Victoria, and Stephen D. Elder. *Becoming a Fundraiser: The Principles and Practice of Library Development*, 2nd ed. Chicago: American Library Association, 2000.

Swan, James. *Fundraising for Small Public Libraries: A How-to-Do-It Manual for Librarians and Trustees*. New York: Neal-Schuman, 1990.

Grants

Barber, Peggy, and Linda Crowe. *Getting Your Grant: A How-to-Do-It Manual for Librarians*. New York: Neal-Schuman, 1993.

Boss, Richard W. *Grant Money and How to Get It: A Handbook for Librarians*. New York: Bowker, 1980.

Gerding, Stephanie, and Pam MacKellar. *Grants for Libraries: A How-to-Do-It Manual.* New York: Neal-Schuman, 2006.

Hall-Ellis, Sylvia D., Doris Meyer, Judy Ann Jerabek, and Frank W. Hoffmann, eds. *Grantsmanship for Small Libraries and School Library Media Centers.* Westport, CT: Libraries Unlimited, 1999.

Information Today and American Library Association. *The Big Book of Library Grant Money, 2006: Profiles of Private and Corporate Foundations and Direct Corporate Givers Receptive to Library Grant Proposals.* Chicago: American Library Association, 2007.

Library Mission

Davies, D. W. *Public Libraries as Culture and Social Centers: The Origin of the Concept.* Metuchen, NJ: Scarecrow, 1974.

Lancaster, F. W. *If You Want to Evaluate Your Library.* Champaign: University of Illinois, Graduate School of Library and Information Science, 1988.

Reed, Sally Gardner. *Making the Case for Your Library: A How-to-Do-It Manual.* New York: Neal-Schuman, 2001.

Wallace, Linda K. *Libraries, Mission, and Marketing: Writing Mission Statements That Work.* Chicago: American Library Association, 2004.

Marketing

De Saez, Eileen Elliott. *Marketing Concepts for Libraries and Information Services.* New York: Neal-Schuman, 2002.

Fisher, Patricia H., Marseille M. Pride, and Ellen G. Miller. *Blueprint for Your Library Marketing Plan: A Guide to Help You Survive and Thrive.* Chicago: American Library Association, 2005.

Ford, Gary T., ed. *Marketing and the Library.* New York: Haworth, 1984.

Franklin, Linda Campbell. *Display and Publicity Ideas for Libraries.* Jefferson, NC: McFarland, 1985.

Liebold, Louise Condak. *Fireworks, Brass Bands, and Elephants: Promotional Events with Flair for Libraries and Other Nonprofit Organizations.* Phoenix: Oryx, 1986.

Siess, Judith A. *The Visible Librarian: Asserting Your Value with Marketing and Advocacy.* Chicago: American Library Association, 2003.

Walters, Suzanne. *Library Marketing That Works.* New York: Neal-Schuman, 2004.

Weingand, Darlene E. *Future-Driven Library Marketing.* Chicago: American Library Association, 1998.

———. *Marketing/Planning Library and Information Services.* Westport, CT: Libraries Unlimited, 1999.

Wolfe, Lisa A. *Library Public Relations, Promotions, and Communications: A How-to-Do-It Manual for Librarians.* New York: Neal-Schuman, 2005.

Wood, Elizabeth J., and Victoria Young. *Strategic Marketing for Libraries: A Handbook.* Westport, CT: Greenwood, 1989.

Woodward, Jeannette A. *Creating the Customer-Driven Library: Building on the Bookstore Model.* Chicago: American Library Association, 2004.

Media

Blake, Barbara Radke, and Barbara L. Stein. *Creating Newsletters, Brochures, and Pamphlets: A How-to-Do-It Manual.* New York: Neal-Schuman, 1992.

Jurewicz, Lynn, and Todd Cutler. *High Tech, High Touch: Library Customer Service through Technology.* Chicago: American Library Association, 2003.

Kalfatovic, Martin R. *Creating a Winning Online Exhibition: A Guide for Libraries, Archives, and Museums.* Chicago: American Library Association, 2002.

Statz, Sarah R. *Public Speaking Handbook for Librarians and Information Professionals.* Jefferson, NC: McFarland, 2003.

Wilson, A. Paula. *Library Web Sites: Creating Online Collections and Services.* Chicago: American Library Association, 2004.

Online Bookselling

Mould, Michael E. *Online Bookselling: A Practical Guide with Detailed Explanations and Insightful Tips.* Odessa, FL: Aardvark, 2006.

Windwalker, Stephen. *Selling Used Books Online: The Complete Guide to Bookselling at Amazon's Marketplace and Other Online Sites.* Belmont, MA: Harvard Perspectives, 2002.

Partnering

Lynch, Sherry, Shirley Amore, and Jerrie Bethel, eds. *The Librarian's Guide to Partnerships.* Fort Atkinson, WI: Upstart Books, 1999.

Policy Development

American Library Association and Joanne S. Anderson. *Guide for Written Collection Policy Statements.* Chicago: American Library Association, 1996.

Bromley, Rebecca. *The Public Library Manager's Forms, Policies, and Procedures Handbook with CD-ROM.* New York: Neal-Schuman, 2004.

Cassell, Kay Ann. *Developing Public Library Collections, Policies, and Procedures: A How-to-Do-It Manual for Small and Medium-Sized Public Libraries.* New York: Neal-Schuman, 1991.

Nelson, Sandra, and June Garcia. *Creating Policies for Results: From Chaos to Clarity.* Chicago: American Library Association, 2003.

Public Library Association. *PLA Handbook for Writers of Public Library Policies.* Chicago: American Library Association, 1993.

Shuman, Bruce A. *Library Security and Safety Handbook: Prevention, Policies, and Procedures.* Chicago: American Library Association, 1999.

Smith, Mark. *Neal-Schuman Internet Policy Handbook for Libraries.* New York: Neal-Schuman, 1999.

Staffing

Cohn, John M., and Ann L. Kelsey. *Staffing the Modern Library: A How-to-Do-It Manual.* New York: Neal-Schuman, 2005.
Smith, Mark L., and Julie Beth Todaro. *Training Library Staff and Volunteers to Provide Extraordinary Customer Service.* New York: Neal-Schuman, 2006.